PARENTS BEWARE OF THE DIGITAL DEMON

PARENTS BEWARE OF THE DIGITAL DEMON

MALAVIKA KAPUR

Published by
Renu Kaul Verma
Vitasta Publishing Pvt Ltd
2/15, Ansari Road, Daryaganj
New Delhi-110 002
info@vitastapublishing.com

वत्स an imprint of Vitasta Publishing

ISBN 978-81-948200-3-1

First Edition 2021

MRP ₹450

Cover and layout by Somesh Kumar Mishra
Printed by Vikas Computer and Printers

Contents

Preface

> It rots the sense in the head!
> It kills imagination dead!
> It clogs and clutters up the mind!
> It makes a child so dull and blind!
> He can no longer understand!
> A fantasy, a fairyland!
> His brain becomes as soft as cheese!
> His powers of thinking rust and freeze!
> He cannot think – he only sees!
>
> —*Roald Dahl*

What on earth is our favourite writer talking about? It is about the impact of that time's (in the 1940s) new technology gadget, the Television! I, as a child psychologist, endorse his view. At present I am concerned with the impact Internet of Things (IoT) and Artificial Intelligence (AI) have on developing minds and brains.

I was an avid fan of science fiction as a youngster. Isaac Asimov, Arthur C Clarke and others of the genre held me spell bound. I truly believed in Asimov's three laws of Robotics.

Isaac Asimov's Three Laws of Robotics

i. A robot may not injure a human being or, through inaction, allow a human being to come to harm.

ii. A robot must obey orders given by human beings, except where such orders would conflict with the First Law.

iii. A robot must protect its own existence as long as such protection does not conflict with the First or Second Law.

I truly believed the above laws to be sacrosanct as the Oath of Hippocrates is in the practice of medicine. Despite the attempts by the evil forces to destroy the world order, the good forces invariably won. How naïve I was to believe in it! I also plead guilty of enjoying horror novels of the genre of MR James to Stephen King.

Mary Shelly was prescient about the future of science when she wrote her novel, *Frankenstein.* She predicted the dangers of scientific curiosity meddling with the natural order of the world. The horror stories were exciting to read but one always identified with the victims empathically and the reader was happy and relieved when the aggressors or the evil ones met a bad end.

In stark contrast, in the present genre of novels or movies, the excitement of horrific deeds is with the perpetrator and the victims only provide joy to the aggressor. Most of the games or events representing victory are based on shooting, killing and destroying the so-called enemy. Identification of the reader or viewer now rests with the aggressor. There is not even a single ray of hope or empathy for the victims.

In these days of bystander apathy to witnessing pain in a road accident, there is no evidence of empathy, compassion and spontaneous helpful behaviour. Bystanders are thrilled to be able to video record and share their excitement and joy of having witnessed something horrific! Enjoyment of inflicting pain has taken over the humane emotion of empathy and compassion.

I do not propose this to be a compendium of all the knowledge available at this time of the dangers of IoT and AI. I choose some research findings and guidelines for reducing this danger. I do not aim at cataloguing notorious school shootings and murders by young children and youth, sensationally described on all media outlets. Nor do I propose to give an overview of all the available literature, be it Indian, Asian or Western on the worldwide web. *The emphasis here is on Indian experiences in schools, child guidance centres and interactions with parents.*

In the 1990s, I saw a case of an adolescent girl who had 'affective disorder' and was addicted to TV programmes with warrior men and women, with obsession about a particular hero indulging in violent acts resulting in lot of blood and gore. I had thought it to be an isolated case. It is not uncommon in clinical practice to find the latest technological ideology or practice getting embedded in active psychotic ideation of a patient. For example, a large number of paranoid patients harbour suspicions based on their belief that these reached them through TV, radio or sound waves or aliens. As a commonsense advice for this particular patient, the family was told to curtail her TV viewing. She recovered after being on anti-psychotic drugs and was back to school.

We had no inkling at that time about television viewing, which we thought as an incidental finding. It took us some years to link child mental health and learning problems to *screen time.*

On the other hand, I have been working for almost three decades in the remote rural areas and in tribal belts in Karnataka in the government and tribal schools. These, typically, were with poor infrastructure, paucity of funding and very scarce number of teachers, that too with poor training. This is when I had the 'Eureka' moment. As promoted by advances in research on

Developmental Psychology, and my own experience as a home schooled happy child, I realised that children can be their own resource. I knew it in my heart of hearts. Now I had evidence. I started focusing on Child-Centred Play Way method as a pedagogic tool and adopted it in over 30 schools with more than 4,000 children. I followed the renowned educationist Prof Yash Pal Sharma's dictum, 'Learn from children what to teach them'. Finally, I have found a replicable, successful, child-centric model for poor countries where the children are indeed our sole resource.

How does one link the Digital Demon to child development, mental health and education?

This is where I attempt to bridge gaps between the three domains. Screen time negates attachment and bonding while 'actual quality time' is only promoted by the family and friends through play, reading and talking.

Indian teachers adopt mostly teacher-centred, authoritative and punitive approach where rote learning and memorising is emphasised and punishment is a norm. The child has no scope for creativity or play or to interact with teachers. Internet, like a traditionally followed way, also uses the top down method despite claims to be an interactive process. It 'dishes out', 'gives', 'serves' programmes. With the use of techno-centric and the traditional teacher-centric methods, children are doomed to become poor learners.

I hope that this book sheds some light on this vast area, and especially sensitises adults to their ignorance about the great potential children have for learning about themselves, others and the world, their ability to communicate and through empathy, form bonding and attachment with family and the society. Parents need to pick up the skills of keen observation from the young children and learn from them how to make the world a better place to live in.

Let me also add a word of caution. It is but natural, in a technologically-advancing and changing world, that at times of confinement and crisis, when there are restrictions on the so far limitless outdoors, mobile phones and TV are the gadgets people resort to, to – what is known in popular parlance as 'pass time' – overcome boredom.

However, restrictions on the *outdoors* should also make every individual realise how precious this 'outdoor' is and how we need to make the most use of it – by playing, walking, running outdoors, rather than sitting with a net-enabled gadget or just sit out, doing nothing.

As we discuss the positive and negative impact of Internet globalisation, suddenly we are facing a tragedy of unknown magnitude in 2020. As we go to press, we face a grim double jeopardy of the exponential growth of Covid-19 followed by a global lockdown and of an explosion of on line platforms, both learning and working platforms!

In this context, it is interesting to recall an expert opinion. On 17 March 2020, the American Academy of Paediatrics published a statement in response to the corona virus pandemic that reflected a somewhat different approach to what it has been saying in the past years on screen time. The statement acknowledged that kids' screen media use 'will likely increase' during the corona virus pandemic, but the Academy did not offer any alternate time limits. Instead, the statement stressed that screen time limits 'are still important' and urged parents to 'preserve offline experiences'.

So how do we go about it? As we agonise over it, art and activity experts Ericka Chang and Tracy Wilkinson offer us the following suggestions.

Follow the 3 Cs they advise: the CHILD, the CONTENT and the CONTEXT.

'And let down your guard', they tell the parents.

Then they proceed to tell us that there has been 60 per cent increase in viewing according to various sources, putting out data in the month of April 2020. From the very strict time limits to 'it is free for all regardless of the hours of the day'.

Guidelines have been deliberately withheld so that the parents don't feel guilty about not adhering to it. What the child watches, we need to know. But we know our children. A fearful child should not be exposed to violent visuals. A child who loves music, dance or art can engage in it. This is where the parents' role becomes important. Quality matters more than the quantity in deciding the content. Get the content description from reputable institutions such as PBS, Commonsense and so on. Please choose slow-paced media like Mr Rogers (shows by the US TV personality Fred Rogers) than fast-paced visuals which tend to over stimulate the developing brain. For older kids, the games which require some aspects of socialisation is preferred but violent games are to be avoided.

No such categorisation is available yet for Indian shows for children and programmes shown on Indian television channels, both Indian and foreign. Yet Indian parents need to be equally alert as screen time for Indian children too has increased due to the pandemic. The app-based games made available on smart phones are also not categorised.

Context is important. You can interact and participate in what children are doing. This enhances their self esteem. But, if you use their screen time to Zoom into your own work, it may not be helpful. The child should not feel you are more interested in something else, which you may be. Watching a programme together on baking and later on baking or cooking with the child, in your kitchen is a productive innovation.

You may use the joint screen time as a great experience of rediscovering your relationships, your children and discover their own skills at these difficult times.

—Malavika Kapur
June 2020

Acknowledgements

I thank all the children who made my life a joyous one and enabled me to learn a great deal about them, that do not exist in books. Nor can I Google it. I thank all the parents who shared their experiences and wisdom with us.

I am deeply indebted to all my child counselors, who enabled us at the Child Guidance Centre of Prasanna Counselling Centre provide free services for the past fifteen years. I share their wisdom with you. I individually thank Geetha A, Vatsala Prasad, Sheela Kamath, Sindhu Karanth, Rajalakshmi Gopal Rao, Arathi Rao, Veena Suresh, Anitha Sudhir, Nisha Shah and Sujatha Reddy of our Child Guidance Centre and Namitha Kumar, formerly of NIAS for their contributions. All of them have contributed the different vignettes given in the text. My special thanks to Rajalakshmi who worked shoulder to shoulder with me in my past writing efforts and the present one. I owe Edassery Sebastian, formerly of Cyber Cell of the CBI, for sharing a panel discussion with me on Challenges of Digital Parenting, an entire section of that discussion.

I am indebted to the National Institute of Advanced Studies for providing the space and opportunity before I write my books, for my ideas to be tested in the faculty presentations. I acknowledge all open source information, all that is available in Creative Commons, Google, Wikipedia and Wkimedia and the world wide web.

Most of all, I am grateful to Renu Kaul Verma and Papri Sri Raman of Vitasta Publishing Private Limited, New Delhi for supporting all my ventures.

My deep understanding of the fantastic world of children is based on my children, Svapna Sabnis and Sharad Kapur and their respective spouses, Samir and Stella, and my four precious grandchildren for being truly grand! My special thanks to Svapna for her critical reading of the first draft and her support as a paediatrician.

PART I

Introduction

WHAT ARE the normal behaviours of children at different ages is explored in this book. What enhances the overall development and what compromises it, is our quest.

Overall development of an individual includes the seven domains of growth and these are: physical, intellectual, language, emotional, social, moral and sexual development. Unless we know how children's brains and minds develop and work, we cannot understand what leads to optimum development.

There are several well-known processes and practices in child development which are based on sound theories supported by a host of empirical findings. Only one among them is the Information Processing Theory. This forms the basis of studies on Artificial Intelligence. Information Processing model proposes that there is a parallel between human and computer learning. This may apply to some extent to learning in adults. Developmental psychology has proven by collating multiple theories – that an infant or a child is not merely a miniature adult and same rules of learning are not common to both. The question here is, whether computer-simulated model promotes or compromises healthy overall development in children.

The pervasive use of Internet of Things (IoT) and Artificial Intelligence (AI) in everyday life, at home, school and the community is very obvious. We are smitten by its power of seduction. These are indeed lethal weapons produced by advertising and marketing strategies of corporate houses and are of very addictive nature. As this menace overcame us gradually and stealthily, without our being aware of it, we can rightly say, our children have been captured by the digital monster.

This book is meant for parents, teachers, and the lay public in general. It focuses on the impact of IoT and AI on infants, children and adolescents while offering digital challenges to the very nature of parenting across the country. The book offers some research evidence and narratives of children, parents and counsellors in creating awareness about the magnitude of the problem, identifying and intervening to fight the monster and reclaim the Indian childhood and adolescence.

In the Western world there is much more awareness and attempts to control screen time.

In India, children have much more access to screen time, without the parents and teachers being even aware about the nature of the destruction, about the demon devouring our children! In the globalised world, being 'responsible netizens' is a much-bandied-about term (perhaps imagined); websites are being showcased as the 'one size fits all solution' or even a panacea for child-safety concerns.

The fact remains that all techno gadgets are created by the adult's own understanding of a child's brain and mind from an adult perspective, which has no bearing on reality. This is especially so as children at different stages are almost like different species as they traverse across the different developmental stages. Also, the 'child' is a 'uniform-brained' creature for the gadget and game developer, film-maker and web designer. *In real life, every child thinks differently, visualises differently, adopts differently, responds differently and internalises differently at different ages.*

What do we owe to our children and adolescents? Something very basic to development of children are good parenting, happy homes and schools; secure and safe environment at home, neighbourhood and schools. Is that too much to ask for or are we taking all the above for granted – both in the developing and developed nations? United Nations advocates the Rights of the Child. But are we protecting them from wars, climate changes, and environmental degradations? Are we protecting them from the digital monster, which possibly is yet another man-made disaster like climate change?

In countries where population is relatively aged, problems are different. For example, in countries like Japan or in the recent times, even in China, where with the one-child policy, there are fewer younger people. But in India, 40 per cent of the population are below 20 years of age and half the population consists of young people. As may be seen in ASER (Annual Status of Education Report) of 2010-2016 across the nation, its surveys found that majority of the 5th standard school-going children have language (regional) and maths skills appropriate for 2nd standard. These findings have been supported by NCERT (National Council of Educational Research and Training) and Pratham.[1] But surprisingly, no attempts have been made by researchers, even at a small scale, to study and provide ways to remedy the looming skill-level disaster.

If this is the status of primary education, how can we expect quality education at higher levels in high school and college? However, this is a reflection only on the government-funded

---

1 Pratham (1995) is an innovative non-profit learning organisation created to improve the quality of education in India.

schools that fall under ASER surveys. We must acknowledge that the social welfare-funded ICDS – Integrated Child Development Services (preschool education) and Ashram schools' education across the country – and the general education system is abysmally poor in quality. This only reflects the state of mass education provided to majority of the Indian children, catering to disadvantaged populations and diverse groups with language, religion, caste, poverty, culture and other such social and economic constraints.

In India, children from the small population of elitist high-income communities alone can afford good preschools, primary and high schools, numerous private schools and professional courses in medicine, engineering, technology and so on and have access to higher education.

Mass education in India for all the children has been obviously neglected due to lack of funding, poor school infrastructure, paucity of teachers and teachers with very poor training, although the populist programme of mid-day meals have magically improved basic nutrition and enrollment in the school systems across India. But the education system in India needs to be turned on its head to take care of the gaps in education.

The decade-old Right to Education Act has not improved conditions.

India is a country that accommodates numerous diversities. These need to be accommodated within the school system. Discrimination along the fault lines of caste, religion, poverty is well recognised but linguistic diversity is at the greatest peril. This is the greatest advantage of a child, if it is capitalised. Languages reflect the cultural diversities of India. Indian children are the most skilled learners of multiple languages. Thus, it is essential that they learn English as a language of upward social mobility and to provide access to the largest bases of knowledge. Yet, the system needs to acknowledge that one's own mother tongue and other regional languages are torch-bearers of respective cultures and sub-cultures.

A child, being a natural linguist, can acquire both English (language of the world) and his own mother tongue (his family culture) and regional language (culture of his State). A Telugu-speaking child and a Hindi-speaking child may be as different as an English-speaking and Spanish- or French-speaking as their mother tongue. English will be the bridge to the world while multiple regional languages are a network of cultures, sub-cultures – in short, the Indian cultural heritage itself.

So, we come to the question as to what happens when globalisation gobbles up the multiplicity of diverse languages, obviously making English the most sought-after language to the exclusion of all the other languages? As precedents we have countries like China, Korea, Japan and Russia who have tenaciously held on to their own languages.

USA has, despite numerous languages spoken by the early immigrants, made English its sole language, divesting the rights of the various immigrants belonging to different religions and language groups and denying them place in the sun. Showing how differently this can be done, India needs to be proud and sustain its linguistic heritage, and yet promote English.

Under the Digital Colonisation process, what is happening to our children is at the core of the debate in this book.

Digital invasion is pervasive across the world, and includes India as well. My hunch is that wherever there is electricity and mobile towers, internet becomes accessible. When we have electricity in every household, we will have a complete digital invasion. For example, take one case study. In a remote village a teenager was being interviewed about his knowledge about what goes on around him. When asked what his father did for living, what was the source of income, the questions drew a blank. He seemed not to care either. But he had a long, animated conversation about his Player Unknown's Battle Grounds (PUBG)* expertise. He lacked all the skills that a 10th grader ought to have had, but had only gaming skills. Is that what we want for our adolescents?

Often, all the global efforts at improving education of the world, persuasively argue that AI will improve the lot of the deprived. One of the studies by Kentaro Toyama, reflected in his book, *Geek Heresy* sites the research done by Microsoft in Bangalore for four years. He came out with the following finding after studying three pilot projects in education, health and development. It was found that *all the pilot projects showed excellent outcomes but failed when these were scaled up.*

Most of the AI achievements are often promoted, based on pilot data.

More the diversity in a population, AI becomes more ineffective in reaching out. In fact, it actually ends up resulting in adverse consequences and collateral damages. Virginia Eubanks, an activist, in 2018 flagged misuses of high-tech tools, calling it aiming to 'Profile, Police and Punish' citizens who do not fit in, calling it *automating inequality* in healthcare and education. Very strong words indeed! The question that naturally arises: Will the new Face Recognition App allow a dictator to have total control over its citizens?

This book aims at examining these aspects of screen time with children. But, the most critical point is that be it child development, mental health, education along with entertainment, they need to be bridged to understand the child. All the four need to be **child-centred**, that it should be in the best interests of the child. The IoT and AI take control of all the above, to the ultimate aim of financial benefit to the creators, service providers. Altruism or child-centeredness become casualties. And it is not even acknowledged by the digital demon.

Developmental phases of childhood and adolescence have been divided into multiple stratas to enable us to do a fine-grained analysis of the differences in all the domains of development. For example, in the first year, it could be one month, three months, six months or nine months. It could be 1 to 2 years or 6-9 years. These phases differ amongst developmental theories, though there is a general consensus on the positive and negative aspect.

For example, Piagetian theory of Cognitive Development occurs in four stages and are as follows:

Stage 1. Sensory – Motor stage, 0 to 2 years. In this stage, the infant learns about his/her body and the world outside through direct interaction through touching, seeing, hearing, smelling and tasting. Though these appear purposeless initially, these gradually become purposive and well-coordinated. There is a constant interaction between the two processes termed accommodation and assimilation. The infant – who mouths every object at hand initially – soon learns what is edible and what is not. Use of the five sensory modalities in the three-dimensional space is very important in this critical phase.

Stage 2. Pre-operational stage, 2 to 7 years. The child does not understand that the same amount of water may appear more in a tall glass when compared to a shallow bowl. Tricky questions such as 'if one shirt takes an hour to dry on a clothesline how long it will take 10 shirts to dry', is difficult for a child to answer at this stage.

Stage 3. Concrete operations stage, 7 to 11 years. In this stage, the basic principles of physics are understood by the child. He can think using mental operations. He can understand the law of conservation, like, the amount of water remains the same irrespective of what container it is in.

Stage 4. Formal operations (abstract thinking) stage, 11 years and above. In this stage the adolescent is as good as an adult in logical operations. In fact, he may even surpass an adult in his abstract thinking and reasoning.

Thus, as the database is massive, developmental stages are numerous, based on the rationale of developmental theories. I have collapsed them into three groups. The first is from zero till the completion of four years, termed 0 to 4; second is from four years till the age he reaches to eleven years and is termed 4 to 11 years; and the third is above 11 years as adolescence, possibly up to 16 or 18 years. Though the child in general is referred to as 'he' in most of the places, it does not mean a boy alone; it may also refer to a girl.

Content of the book is divided into two parts: Part I with 9 chapters and Part II with 6 chapters.

Part I

The first chapter introduces the themes covered in the book, apart from a general introduction, pervasive use of the Internet of Things (IoT) and Artificial Intelligence (AI), the online forces that knowingly or unknowingly expose children and adolescents to unforeseen, insidious, non-observable internal and external dangers.

The productive use of technology has been overtaken by invisible threat to the natural overall development across domains and, in fact, is creating a surge in mental health risk to children.

One cannot deny that screen time does help to enhance some competencies such as analytic abilities, eye and motor coordination and quick reflexes. But on the downside, children are losing out on their communication skills, family and social bonding and capacity for empathy, most importantly self-control. On the other hand, the genie of IoT and AI is out of the bottle, we have no knowledge of how it can be contained.

Chapter 2 focuses on the Nature of the child. The infant at birth is prewired to proceed through the overall developmental trajectories along physical, cognitive language, emotional, social, moral and sexual domains.

Equally, the role of family and society are contributors to this holistic development as well. Indian indigenous health systems have been the earliest pioneers to recognise the 'Scientist in the Crib'. In fact, the foetus is conscious of his environment in the womb and the maternal interaction with the environment. The most important point is that the human brain is at peak level of development in the early years. That is why the need to protect it from technologcal invasions, especially through foetal, infancy and toddler stages.

Chapter 3 focuses on screen time hazards for the very young, that is zero to four years. *Parents' understanding of harmful effects of screen time is abysmally low among the Indian parents.* Research too is very limited except in Korea and China, where the dangers have been flagged and rehabilitation efforts are attempting to deal with the virtual disasters. In this book, many real cases and anecdotal Indian accounts are given. But all the names are fictitious.

Chapter 4 deals with the effect of screen time on children from 4 to 11 years. The child's cognitive and language skills change in these years dramatically and so will the strange power of the screen that holds them in thrall and moves them away from reality. Once again cases, anecdotes and research findings are used to make sense of what is happening to our children on the domains of development. Screen time is a passive activity and affects them differently in various developmental stages. However, the content of what is viewed is more critical than the actual screen time. But the real harm occurs when an increased screen time reduces real time attachment and interaction with the family and leads to academic decline.

Chapter 5 discusses the nature and nurture aspects in the age group 11 and above. Rapid changes occur in all the domains of development, causing significant changes in each domain. They are at risk for mental health issues and compromised development for the individual as well as a group itself. Once again, harm that comes in the way of achieving normal adolescence because of the danger of virtual reality replacing reality is highlighted.

Chapter 6 focuses on mental health, disabilities and the diversities across the nation. Mental health concerns have been totally ignored due to the obsession with the merits of technology. To me, this is my gravest concern, as I, with over five decades of experience as a clinician, am unable to determine quantitatively, the impact of ever-changing virtual reality on children and unravel the 'clinical manifestations' in the child and adolescence across the country and how to help them.

For this reason, we have given several case illustrations in the three age groups, namely 0 up to 4 years, 4 up to 11 years and 11 years and above. Adverse effects vary enormously in the three age groups. The qualitative deterioration in a child's development is quite obvious, but we are yet unable to quantify the scale of harm a gadget-dependent life-style does to a child.

Chapter 7, the title being 'Nature of the Beast' refers to the tech giants, labelling them as beasts or monsters. This is likely to be the most controversial chapter as most people believe that technology has solution to all the problems of mankind.

The author on the other hand believes that immense harm has been forced on humanity, particularly on the children. Technology causes disintegration of the family, society and cultures across the world, ultimately aiming at removing all the diversities. Total move is away from reality to virtual reality. This I see as the end of this civilisation as we knew it. Our children are the unintended victims of this calamity.

A package given to overcome cyber crime against children is provided by cyber crime expert E Sebastian in a simple format and is included in this chapter.

Chapter 8 explores the roles of advertising and marketing in the children's world, specifically in the IoT and AI realms. Merchants from times immemorial have enticed customers to buy their products. Commercial exploitation has increased to an enormous extent, especially on the online modes. It is essential for all of us to be aware of its deception and guard ourselves and our children against it. Advertisers are amoral, greedy and exploit us and we should be wise to their efforts.

Chapter 9 deals with the collusion of technology with education. Basically, both collude in advertising and running a profitable business called 'educational technology'. This is to the detriment of education, empowering neither teachers nor children. It makes the teacher dependent on technology. The education is top down and not child-centred and play-based. The child contributes nothing to the process of learning, as the interactive modes are predetermined by the corporate designers.

Part II

Consists of six chapters and deals with awareness creation and intervention possibilities for the three age groups mentioned in the earlier chapters.

These include case studies, anecdotes and research findings. The symptoms range from Autism-like syndromes, delayed speech and language development, rising incidents of Attention Deficit Hyperactivity Disorder (ADHD), learning disorder, aggression, violence and psychoses. All these are in addition to uprooting of other emotional, social and educational support systems. But possibly, back to basics and back to nature, is a way to go. Even if this is only partly successful.

Chapter 10 covers interventions for 0 to 4-year old children. The impact of over-stimulation or under-stimulation on the developing brain is clearly described. Specific problems typical to this stage, such as language delays, autistic features and attention deficit disorders are highlighted.

In chapter 11 interventions cover 4 to 11 years age range. Focus is on cognitive development, attachment and bonding with the family, language and communication with the family and others as well as social development. This is a critical phase for the optimal development in an integrated fashion.

Chapter 12 covers the crucial period of adolescence. Academic performance takes precedence in the Indian ethos. It overshadows creativity, healthy psychosocial development and comes at the cost of emotional wellbeing.

Physiological and psychological changes play a major role in family and peer bonding and one's relation to the society. The adolescents run into risks on the internet which include falling prey to pedophiles, drug addiction, pornography and sex sites, depression with suicidal rumination, anxiety with occasional manifestation of psychotic or obsessive features. These wreak havoc on the families as well as the society.

Chapter 13 provides general guidelines for parents based on various advisory bodies as well as individual experts. These are offered for different age groups and linked to the developmental requirements.

Chapter 14 directs some Approaches to Solutions. This adopts a bottom up than top down approach. With children it is a Child-centred Play Way Approach. In adolescence, it is activity-based but adolescent-centred, as well as through peer learning which experience shows, has contributed a great deal to learning. Hence promotion of old-fashioned family and societal values, where pro-social behaviour is considered to be of utmost importance is recommended.

Chapter 15 is Reflections. All healthy interactions are embedded in empathy. Screen time addiction can never be by itself targeted for intervention. The whole and complete healing of the child needs to be worked upon. It has to deal out holistic and supportive therapeutic intervention. How these can be conducted by parent group support is described with illustration of such efforts in our Child Guidance Centre.

---

* It is not for nothing that the Government of India has banned the game PUBG in India since 2 September 2020. With more than 40 per cent of the country's population under 30 years, PUBG has been time and again proven to be a fatal addiction, with the Indian media reporting at least one casualty every week due to young people playing this game. It also banned the app Tik Tok, along with 250 other addictive applications on phones and computers.

The GoI has also banned the game Blue Whale.

Oestensibly, the bans came because all these games and apps were China-made products. Tencent, the company providing this game, lost nearly $42B USD in market value in just two days since the announcement of the India ban. Tencent also lost $6B in market capitalisation when India decided to ban Tik Tok on June 29.

A casual tracking of the Indian media for the last three years reveals the nature of the beast – the violence, the suicides, the heart failures and associated depression and agreesion that adolescents are subject to because of these gadget-supported activities. What hapens to younger children is far less recorded in Indian media.

https://esportsobserver.com/indian-stakeholders-pubg-mobile/

Nature of the Child

DEVELOPMENT OF the brain and development of the body starts in the womb of the mother. In the indigenous health systems such as Ayurveda, Unani, Siddha, Tibetan and folk medicines, as practised all over traditional Indian homes, childcare begins with the care of the pregnant woman.

What is termed as 'embryology' in modern times is basically a physiological understanding of the growth of the embryo, leading to the foetus being considered as just a growing organism that needs to be nourished. It is not attributed any psychological qualities in the Western healthcare systems, unlike the indigenous health systems.

My work on childcare in the indigenous health care reveals (Kapur 2016) the following:

Unlike Western health care systems, the indigenous systems have all highlighted that the foetus is indeed initially conscious of pain and pleasure sensations. Later on, it is attributed the dawn of cognition as well.

In the Western world, emergence of consciousness, emotions and cognition in the foetus were unknown. Only in the recent decades, the foetus is acknowledged to be reacting to psychological changes in the mother with EEG (Electro-Encephalogram) and ECG (Electro-Cardiogram) disturbances. The movements of the foetus are activated by music, maternal distress, anxiety or happiness. This has encouraged the parents to talk and sing to the baby in the womb. Maternal alcohol addiction during pregnancy is known to produce 'foetal alcohol syndrome' in the newborn infant, leading to symptoms of withdrawal of alcohol or drugs if the mother is a drug addict.

The pregnant mother and the baby in the womb are considered as a symbiotic unit in the indigenous health tradition. The treatment for the newborn, as long as she is breastfed, is given to the mother and never directly to the baby. The mother has an important role to play in promoting healthy mind and body in the baby. After the birth, the newborn continues to interact with the physical and psychological environments as s/he did in the foetal environment.

The Nature of Brain Development

From birth to the age of two years is most critical to brain development. For example, infant's brain weight is approximately 400 grams. Yet it is already 25 per cent of the weight of an adult's brain. A six-month old's brain weighs half as much as that of an adult. By the age of two years, it will be as much as 75 per cent of an adult brain. Thus, the first two years is the most critical time for brain development.

These are not mere speculations – as we may suppose – just because these are described in the indigenous systems. These have been supported in the area of developmental psychology.

The *Scientist in the Crib* (Gopnik et al 1999) is one of the books that opens our eyes to the enormous potential of the infant's brain. Research on children is not easy because they cannot report their thoughts or feelings. But by systematic observation of their behaviour, one can gain insights into their minds.

There are different methods to study babies. Children were studied using baby biographies by Socrates, Darwin and Piaget. The other methods are observation, both naturalistic and experimental, time sampling, meticulous record keeping, baby diary, audio and video recording, psycho physiological readings and also conversations with infants, babies and children.

Children need to be studied cross-sectionally and longitudinally to get better understanding. Cross-sectionally, thousands of babies can be studied using the above methods at one point of time. The same group of children may also be studied longitudinally from 0 to 16 years or in infancy, childhood, adolescence and so on. Both the methods have contributed to our understanding of developmental psychology.

Emerging Insights in Developmental Psychology

How Do Children Learn about Things in the External World?

For example, newborns prefer bold stripes, clear contours, bright, moving and 3D objects. A day-old baby imitates facial expression. This is included in the Piagetian phases of cognitive development in handling external objects through the processes of accommodation and assimilation, simultaneously going through stages of cognitive development and understanding object constancy vs that which is out of sight but exists.

How Children Learn about People – You and Me?

Earlier in the West, the newborns were believed to be without vision, thinking, sensation or pain. But now it has discovered that even a foetus can sense mother's physical and psychological states in the womb itself. Recorded eye movements of paying close attention to a part or whole, duration of attention, losing interest etc., are observed at birth. Even the very young show preference to human face and voice, especially that of the mother, and can differentiate a mask from the mother's face and respond only to the latter.

Other Minds: Thinking and Emotions

- At one month: An experimenter has a flashlight on his forehead on the first visit. During the second visit, a week later the infant looks only at the forehead and obviously notices the absence of the flash light. At one month the infant clearly remembers an event a week earlier.
- By one year: the child can point to things, looking at objects you point to, reading expressions of liking or disgust, and know what you can do with objects.
- By two years: the child can understand that others are like me. He can learn by imitation and have empathy.
- At three: they experience different desires and emotions. They can understand deception and they may deliberately reach for forbidden objects. They may do it to attract attention or actually to provoke adults.

By the age of two, language skills emerge on the horizon. This makes the empirical research even more challenging. Cognitive development occurs in stages along with language development, from a very primitive stage of logic to a very sophisticated one, as highlighted by Jean Piaget (1929). Piaget based his four phases of cognitive development based on observation of his own three children. He then set up experiments to validate them. His studies of both cognitive and language development provide ample proof that a newborn arriving in the world is 'prewired' for understanding and responding to the world and reciprocally communicating and responding to it.

What is the Nature of the Child?

Under child development, nature of the child is highlighted as 'the scientist in the crib' and not born as a 'clean slate' at birth. He is endowed with predisposition to facilitate cognitive, language, emotional, social and moral development soon after birth. Children are also endowed with temperament which represents innate emotionality. The brain development is almost equal to that of adults by the time a child is seven years old, though it is at peak by three years. But the approach to empowered learning depends on child-centred play-way method and not teacher-centred rote learning method.

The next concern is that of mental health problems interfering with the child's school achievement. There are Developmental Disorders, Attention Deficit Hyperactivity Disorder (ADHD), Disorders of Emotion and Conduct (or Internalising and Externalising Disorders) and Specific Learning Disorders (SLD). At adolescence, the teenagers, in addition to the above disorders, may have specific concerns of drug, alcohol and internet abuse, sexuality and gender identity issues as well. These disorders are due to multiple causes and need to be treated accordingly.

A brief note on Mental Health of Children and Adolescents:

Developmental Problems and Disorders

These may manifest as poor coordination and clumsiness, delays and disorders in speech and language, bed wetting/ daytime wetting or present as Specific Learning Disorders (difficulties).

Attention Deficit Hyperactivity Disorder (ADHD)

It is characterised by over activity, impulsivity and attention deficit. It begins early when the child starts to walk, and over-activity comes down as the child grows older but impulsivity and attentional problems tend to continue. An important question is: whether the three features are present in all situations or only in certain situations. If it is only in certain situations, it can be managed with changing the situation when it occurs. In addition, ADHD has impact on language development and causes problems with teachers and other children. It may also manifest as Learning Difficulties.

Specific Learning Disorders (SLD)

Generally, these children have average or above average intelligence, but have difficulties only in Reading, Writing or Maths. They have reasonably good or average schooling. They have no visual, auditory or other disabilities. The learning problems have always been there and not of recent onset.

Please note that schools with paucity of teachers and infrastructure, poor academics *reflects systems failure* and not SLD in the child.

Emotional disorders are characterised by sad, quiet, withdrawn, fearful, anxious, and shy children. At times, these disorders are present with refusal to go to school. These are also termed 'internalising disorders'. They are mostly distressing to the child.

Conduct disorders are characterised by disruptive behaviour, physical and verbal aggression, indulging in bullying, stealing and lying. Disobedience and oppositional behaviour are frequently seen. These are termed 'externalising disorders' and are distressing to others. In many cases, both emotion and conduct disorders may coexist in the same child.

All the disorders often are due to multiple causes. These could be, difficult home environment, difficult school environment, difficult temperament or cognitive difficulties. There may be overlapping of disorders in the same child. The same cause may produce different disorders as well.

Find out the causes and try to help by **identification, referral** and **management.**

Child Development

Promotion of Overall Development and Mental Health – PLAY is the Key.

- Promoting Overall development of children through Play.
- Identify, refer and manage mental health problems.
- Adopt a **child-centred** approach instead of a teacher-centred approach.
- In short, a change of mindset to see the children as they really are and not as *we believe* they are.

There are several views about the nature of the child among adults including psychologists, philosophers, parents and teachers. One is that the mind of the newborn is like a 'clean slate' (Tabula Rasa) by John Locke. The infant's mind is a 'blooming buzzing confusion', William James, the most eminent of the psychologists before our time believed. But all the above assumptions were speculative.

There were psychologists who experimented with infants, babies and children (often unethically) to prove their hypotheses. This school of thought was termed 'behaviour or learning theory' approach. These so-called scientific experiments by BF Skinner (1953) gained foothold all over the world. For example, Skinner claimed he could train any child to become a genius or an idiot.

Learning principle was applied by Watson (1930) to have introduced fear for furry objects by associating with loud sounds in little Albert. Learning principles do have a role in bringing about desired changes in behaviour.

Innate predisposition is equally important for healthy development of the child.

This view is substantiated by research on the innate potential of the child. Is the child a scientist in the crib? Those who have observed and studied the very young indeed propose this to be true.

Cognitive Development

Then came Jean Piaget (1896-1980) in the present century who observed his own three children and kept a journal on their activities through their entire childhood. He set up simple experiments to test out if his theories could be proved or they were only speculations. He also added naturalistic observation as a method in addition to simple experiments. He described in detail the behaviour of each child and drew conclusions based on them.

He spoke of four stages of cognitive development which revealed essentially, development of logic. These are pre-causal stage, pre-operational stage, stage of concrete operations and stage of abstract reasoning which is the final stage which the child shares with the adults. Piaget is the most influential thinker in study of cognitive development even today.

Vygotsky (1896-1934) added the dimension of culture that the infant imbibes from his natural environment which consists of parents, siblings and family, the inner circle. In 1934, Lev Vygotsky added a social component to cognitive development that consists of two processes. These are internalisation and the zone of proximal (physical closeness) development. He proposed that development proceeds from the environment (physically close or spatially distant) being internalised. It is more social than biological. Much of a child's learning occurs through his interactions with his environment that he internalises. But the adults around fail to observe and believe that children see nothing, hear nothing and understand nothing, be it at home or in the school. They fail to capitalise on this immense potential for learning in children. For example, one may learn great deal about a child when taken on a field trip than on direct questioning in the classroom. Child-centred play is an ideal tool to understand the creative potential of children. He then adds the social dimensions to himself in relation to others. He becomes a social being. It is important for a child to be a part of the society.

Language Development

Chomsky's (1968) observation that children are 'prewired' for language acquisition even before birth, is a major revelation in the understanding of acquisition of language. In contrast, the behaviourists held that we teach children the language. The studies were mostly on single language acquisition. Much of the Euro-centric language literature described language acquisition along these lines. But these did not explain how such rapid word acquisition occurred in the very young children.

The study of language acquisition in India with diversity of languages, produced path-breaking research on multilingualism and language acquisition. A normal child in a joint family setting may spontaneously talk in multiple languages, depending on the language of the adult he is speaking to, by the age of two or three years. This supports Chomsky's contention that infants are prewired for language acquisition. He suggested there exists an innate grammatic structure in the brain, which is universal. Actual language acquisitions take place around it. If exposed to multiple languages early, it is an advantage.

Language, in addition, carries with it the cultural heritage of the region. Language is the transmitter of the cultural heritage as well. Multiple language acquisition, in fact, enriches the very nature of cognitive development as well. The first six months in a pre-verbal child determines how effectively and quickly the child would acquire language, so that the child is ready to acquire languages, he is exposed to, with ease.

While cognitive and language developments remain in the fore front, temperament is a construct that has failed to catch up with the progress made in these areas. Temperament is the psychological trait, which is inborn, which points to individual differences in the emotionality of the children.

Development of Emotions

Charles Darwin, the father of theory of evolution, actually observed his own infants with the same keen scientific curiosity he studied the species of animals. He discovered that when lemon juice is squeezed on to the lips of the infant, the facial expression indicated that it was disliked. He suggested that infants do express some basic emotions very early in life.

Thomas and Chess (1977) spoke of children of three types: those who are good and easy to manage, difficult to manage and slow to learn. On the other hand, an ancient Indian construct on innate psychological disposition is termed *Triguna*. It consists of *Satvik* (happy and good social disposition and sensitivity and empathy towards others), *Rajasik* (very active, intemperate mood, aggressive and dynamic disposition) and *Tamasik* (laid back and emotionally distant).

Satvik nature is considered the ideal one as it makes the child less vulnerable to stress, competent and born with caring attitude to others. These can undergo changes according to the child-rearing practices. An irritable child can be soothed by an affectionate caring mother or aggravated by an irritable and neurotic mother. The inborn dispositions may be modified by supportive or adverse environments (Kapur 2016).

The brain of the newborn is exposed to multiple sensations in contrast to the quiet floating in the amniotic fluid in the womb. At birth, there is sudden exposure to bright lights, loud sounds, strange tastes and smells. But most important is the tactile experience – or the baby's skin all over the body being exposed to cold or warmth. Comfort of being close to the warm body of the mother is the first total experience in addition to all the other sensations. This is considered the most *essential experience* for the newborn. In the animal world too, baby animals seek physical closeness to the mother.

Several studies have shown that this is essential for normal emotional development. The Harlow (1958) study shows importance of physical proximity in baby monkeys, as leading to attachment. John Bowlby's (1969) observation of institutionalised children show, though taken good care of by nurses round the clock, with abundance of toys, good food, these young children grow up to be emotionally distant and withdrawn. He coined the term 'maternal deprivation' and 'maternal bonding'. For normal attachment to develop, bonding with the caretaker is needed, and is both physical and psychological. The critical period for it to occur is between 9 and 36 months. Other pioneer works like that of Mary Ainsworth (1981) described attachment behaviour while clinging to the mother as a main characteristic. She noted 'separation anxiety', if removed from mother's presence. She also noted 'stranger anxiety' during this period. The mother-child interaction is characterised by:

- Close affectionate bond between the mother and child starts before birth and continues thereafter. This is strengthened by physical closeness, breast feeding and display of affection.
- There is eye contact between the two.
- There is constant verbal and non-verbal communication even before the infant can speak. Communication begins much before in the child – very early in infancy – and is often understood only by the mother.
- The child is constantly exposed to visual, hearing, tasting, touching and smelling experiences of the mother and environment around.
- Soon bonding and attachment becomes generalised to others around like father, sibling and other family members and even pets.
- The child is a quick learner and learns by observation and mimicry, as well as instruction of right or wrong or yes and no.

- Before 36 months, during the peak development of the brain, all the above factors enhance normal development. This leaves us with a question, can the above whole gamut of experiences be replaced by Artificial Intelligence, robot nannies or even cell phones?

Why is 0 up to 4 years the most significant for overall development of the brain and mind of the child?

Educated parents of higher socio-economic classes have always attempted to provide their children with the best they can offer in terms of environment to especially promote cognitive and language development. Such experiments deal with combination of latest facts as well as conventional wisdom. Baby Einstein DVDs, Flash Cards, Montessori approach, superior educational toys methods have been tried. None of them conclusively proved to be effective.

Social experiments such as 'Head Start'[2] for disadvantaged pre-schoolers have shown to be effective to some extent. However, more than the individual parenting inputs, more success has to be evidenced.

The 30-million word gap between the children of professionals and working class in the USA was first flagged by Hart and Risley in 1995. They studied 42 families and reported a 30-million word gap between the children of the above two groups at the age of three and the difference persisted even after four years. The study claimed widespread attention only in 2003. This led to numerous replicated and evaluative studies. The study had its share of criticisms. It is interesting that the

2 Head Start is a programme of the United States Department of Health and Human Services that provides comprehensive early childhood education, health, nutrition, and parent involvement services to low-income children and families. The programme's services and resources are designed to foster stable family relationships, enhance children's physical and emotional well-being, and establish an environment to develop strong cognitive skills.

psychologists, sociologists and economists studying the social class distinctions in language development of three-year-olds brought out the notion of 30-million words advantages for children of affluent families. But the lessons learnt were pretty simple.

- Talk to your children
- Read to them
- Play with them

While 30-million words may be an exaggeration, but the adoption of the above three methods have shown significant improvement in future school achievements of the children. This evidence has social policy implications for countries like India. It is better to put in place the **three preferred practices** into operation across the nation.

In India, where there is illiteracy, can the above work? I can assure you it can. Our illiterate population, mostly in rural and tribal regions, have honed the oral tradition to perfection. These could be stories, songs, lullabies, dances and word games reflecting the cultural heritage of each ethnic group. All we need to do is to make them into preferred practices.

Create awareness among the parents about the above three principles. Even illiterate and disadvantaged parents can talk and tell stories, as it happened in all the ancient cultures. Story telling has been an important aspect of all ancient cultures apart from art, music and dance. All the above art forms may have emerged from play of young children. Some linguists believe that even language may have first occurred with human infants, with the utterance of mama and dad!

Screen Time Hazards and the Very Young

0 to 4 Years

OFTEN PARENTS use television (TV) or video as a substitute to actually being with the child or use these as virtual nannies.

In India, most urban parents like their young children inside the house rather than playing outdoors. The reasons are many:

- You can keep an eye on them.
- They are physically safe.
- The other children may be of different (lower) social strata, different religion or speak different language and are deemed not to be appropriate choice as playmates.
- Play is considered non-essential and purposeless activity in India as a rule.
- In the urban areas, it is believed that the earlier one starts the child on reading, writing and learning by rote,

the better it is for the child's link to future educational achievement and therefore, learning by rote, writing and reading are essential at very early ages.

- There is a belief that TV or videos are educational.
- Parents of all social strata take pride in their children's acquisition of gadget use skills. Those from the disadvantaged population consider TV and mobiles to be status symbols.

Let us examine the impact of some instances of early childhood (0 to 4 years) exposures to 'screen time'.

Case 1

The first one is the story of a nine-month-old boy called Raja.

His mother was secretary in my office. She asked for my help as I was a psychologist. I asked her what the problem was. The mother said, she was having trouble with her first born. I asked her to describe in detail what was causing her concern.

She said, 'In the evening when we, that is the entire family, settle down to watch TV, Raja would get scared, tremble and then even look nauseous'. I asked the mother, 'Where was the child and what was he doing?', considering that he should be crawling and exploring the room.

She said, 'He sits on my lap when I watch TV. We ask him to watch it too, so that he does not disturb us'.

I asked, 'What programme do you watch?'

She said, 'We watch Tamil movies'. On further probe on their quality, I understood that they were full of fights, blood, gore and with a lot of screaming and shouting. I had to explain to the mother that a nine-month-old would be very frightened by such scenes. She should forgo her TV viewing or get someone to play with the child elsewhere during her TV time. Here is a case where we have the young child made to view inappropriate violent scenes on TV. There were no more episodes with this child when the instructions were followed.

Case 2

Ten year ago, a young grandmother, who worked as a domestic help, while visiting her married daughter, complained to me, 'My grandson does not look at my face when I talk to him or smile at him or make faces to amuse him. He cranes his neck and looks for the TV'. It so happened that the one-year-old child was viewing television with the parents, when they were at home and he spent rest of the time viewing TV with the paternal grandparents. They were especially addicted to TV serials from morning till night. This deprived the one-year-old from any normal communication or play, despite four adults being in the household.

At the time, I did not pay much attention, believing it to be an one-off episode, after instructing the grandmother and the family that the child needs to play and not watch TV. Life changed for this child. This grandmother began to play with him. Even today, he loves his grandmother and is very close to her as she plays and talks to him. Some years later, I came across experiments of TV viewing and its link with violence and aggression.

Some Early Studies on Violence and TV

In the early days of movies across the world, people loved movies, especially blockbusters in India as well as elsewhere in the world. But it was outside the home. In the West, there were strict rules about children not being allowed in, unless it was a children's movie. In India, children were considered part of the family and taken into the movie theaters, regardless of their age. In India, as children, parents and family are considered a single possible symbiotic unit, they shared everything, sleeping together (co-sleeping), eating together late, and keeping late hours for going to sleep. Since movie-viewing was a special occasion, children were taken to the theatre where they either slept or were taken outside when they fussed.

However, the entire scenario changed with the advent of

the technology of television. A number of studies measuring the impact of television viewing in the laboratory and in the field settings, were conducted. The short-term and long-term impact was measured. Some interesting examples came from the USA, Canada and South Africa. Centerwall et al (1994) studied the homicide rates in the three countries before 1945 and after 1974. The study found an increase of more than 90 per cent in violence in these countries.

But with these early crude measures, the impact chronicled may have been biased. However, there has never been any doubt that the impact of unlimited television viewing on children need to be studied without sweeping conclusions; and there is no doubt either that many earlier studies had pointed towards negative impact on children.

Early report of relationship between physical and verbal aggression came from Joy et al (1986) in a study in a small Canadian town which was named 'Notel' before and after the introduction of TV and two towns where TV was not introduced. A cohort of 45 first and second graders was observed for acts of physical aggression. The rates did not change in the control towns after two years. There was, however, a jump of instances of hitting, biting and aggression which increased by 160 per cent in NotelTown.

Eron and Huesman (1984) followed up a group of 875 children in a similar rural area and reported on eight years of TV viewing and predicating serious crimes in men in their 30s.

However, the media lobby of that time effectively countered the above alarming findings, claiming that TV viewing is only one of the factors. It agreed that violence was a 'learnt behaviour' but linked the nature of aggression with the content and not with viewing and said that the 'impact is stage specific' and 'after all, it was only entertainment'.

Today, international and national studies agree on violence promoted by TV, as there is now a large body of evidence. Yet this has not caused any serious concern, especially in India.

The ancient and medieval times were full of strife and violence, but these were limited to geographically small areas and were not witnessed by the entire world. In the ancient times, dramas portraying these events in the epics had their own code of conduct. For example, Bharatha in his *Natyashastra*, between 200 BCE to 200 CE, stipulated that violence, death and blood and gore *are not to be displayed on the stage*. The hero may carry a sword but *shall not stab on the stage!* The oral narrative of the fights or wars will be given by the Suthradhara at the wings or on the centre stage, by way of singing or conversation with the audience. Which means, one could listen to it and imagine it, but there was no 'display' of war action, this could not be seen, only imagined.

All these changed with the advent of early Greek plays. Direct performance on stage of tragedies became a popular trend. However, the impact of this was also geographically limited. Indian audiences learnt of what happened in Troy only after English language came to India. The current cult of *visual portrayal of violence* is global and spreads fast even when it occurs in a remote corner of the world. The seeing of the Iraq war uncensored in the drawing rooms of the world was talk of the town a few decades ago.

What is the impact of lack of this censorship of violence?

Advertising and Marketing

Children love TV jingles.

They keenly observe the advertisement for the unusual movements of the models, attractively packaged toys, even clothes. Very young children are used as role models in these programmes. Multiple times repetition of the advertisement makes a great impact on their brains and minds of those viewing them. We discuss this in more detail in a later chapter.

Some Observations on Peppa and Lmitation

Peppa, or *Peppa Pig*, is a pre-school television programme made in the UK, with 254 episodes. It was first aired on 31 May

XPLORE
MONDAY 11.02.2019

PEPPA EFFECT

Some parents told parenting site Romper that their kids have begun oinking and snorting

Children in the US are now pronouncing certain words with a British accent

COUNTRY OF ORIGIN: UK | NO OF SERIES: 5 | NO OF EPISODES: 254

FIRST AIRED: May 31, 2004

EXFILE

Is your kid speaking like Peppa?

Well it's the 'Year of the Pig' and Peppa is on her way to becoming a full-fledged icon. The British children TV show follows the adventures of two piglets Peppa and her brother George, and her friends. With almost every merchandise under her name — from toys to watches to even temporary tattoos — Peppa is famous. However, parents outside the UK are not very happy as their children are picking up a posh Brit accent all because of her

CHARACTERS

PEPPA PIG
She is the main character of the series and is talkative, whose hobbies include jumping in puddles and playing with her teddy bear
The four year-old wears a red dress and loves going to her playgroup along with her friends

GEORGE PIG
He is Peppa's younger brother. George loves his toy dinosaur, which he pronounces as 'dine saur'
He is two years old and goes to the same playgroup as Peppa

MUMMY PIG AND DADDY PIG
Mummy Pig works from home and is often seen on the computer. Daddy Pig is an architectural engineer

PEPPA'S FRIENDS

EVERYTHING IS NORMAL
A recent study by Uni of Plymouth showed toddlers aren't able to distinguish between that are pronounced differently

20 months
A toddler's accent is by those around them in settings, instead of school or home and from around 20 months, a start to develop their own accent

2004. It won the British Academy Children's Awards for best pre-school animation. The programme has become iconic, with extensive marketing of toys. Peppa is a global phenomenon, popular not only in the UK but also in the USA and other countries. Peppa is a pig and has parents, younger brother and friends. Soon, some parents reported that their kids had begun oinking and snarling after watching the show. Children who view it, adopt typical English accent instead of Scottish, Irish or American accent. There was even a fake news of screaming monsters bursting out of the cartoon and scaring the children viewing Peppa! Peppa is today shown on Indian television too and very popular 16 years later. Can viewer of Peppa recognise a real pig if s/he sees one, many ask.

Progress of AI and Gadget Addiction in India

In the last two years in my world of children, AI has surreptitiously introduced us to new mental health problems in the very young. Some pediatricians and physical therapists have been reporting speech delays in children exposed to iPads and mobiles, even in India.

As pointed out in the earlier chapters, communication needs to be spontaneous, interactive and with real parents, siblings and friends. Instances of 'feeding problem – in the absence of screen time' is on the rise. 'He won't eat otherwise!' is a common complaint among parents of Indian school children.

In recent years, many children have been brought to my Child Guidance Clinic as 'Autistic'. These children have normal attachment and bonding yet some odd and persistent preoccupations, especially addiction to mobile and TV. As a result, inexperienced diagnosticians diagnose 'Autism' in these kids. Then we have cases where the toddler refuses to eat, unless he watches TV or mobile. When the child throws a tantrum, only access to a mobile will stop the tantrum. Despite all these problems, many Indian parents are proud that their kids are addicted to technology.

The following is an incident from the perspective of a grandmother:

Can You Do This?
Case 3

It was when my younger grandson was two years young. Every one of us had our gadgets, using them, whenever we had to. He too wanted his share. Then we decided to give him some coloured balls to watch through YouTube, with an adult by his side.

After watching them, he used to be restless (till then he was happy and active, or at the most, very very active). He expected us to do many things we were even unable to imagine. Once, after watching his ten minutes share of the gadget, he came to me, and pointed at the orange tub at home. I brought it out for him. He went into it, lay down inside and asked me to bring the coloured balls. I fetched a dozen coloured balls from his toy box. He ordered me to pour them into the basin. They didn't cover him, as it had happened on YouTube. It was his anticipation, rather enactment of the show he had witnessed online just then.

He was very upset and I too! I was witnessing the exposure, a regular, continual exposure, to a virtual world. It had converted a happy child's ever-smiling face into a sad, angry, disgusted, helpless countenance with disbelief and disappointment writ large on it. One of the significant figures of his everyday life was an incapable person, helpless, may be a useless granny.

How could he feel secure with her?

With several similar instances, we became more cautious. The child is now three years old and grown. He has learnt to obey us when limits are fixed. Most of the times, he quits the chair, where he sits to watch YouTube on a computer, happily when we say his time is over and goes in search of a new activity. At times, however, he just creeps in when any of us, especially the grandparents, have our mobiles in our hands. The attraction still holds.

Contributed by KG Rajalakshmi

Screen Addiction and Aggression

How does early excessive screen time or interactive AI like Alexa affect young children?

Not long ago, a proud parent told the paediatrician that their one-year-old's first word was 'Alexa'. Globally, preschoolers regularly consult Alexa about choices of dresses to order, stories or songs to listen to. Parents **fail to recognise** that Alexa is taking over parenting. I am sure any parent would be proud to hear the word 'Mamma' or 'Daddy' as the first words. The mother should be the first confidante to be trusted by a young child.

A dictum to be recognised and noted is that screen time induces 'detachment' from reality. Real death can be traumatic. In contrast, on the screen, death is exciting. For example, does a four-year-old understand what is death? They understand it differently at different stages of cognitive development.

For a 0 to 18-month old, 'out of sight is out of mind'. Then at the next stage, s/he may see it only as person not being active and not moving and so on. Slowly, with adults explaining to them, they begin to comprehend death. Indeed, death and aggression on screen comes in the way of normal bonding and attachment with the mother, father and siblings and even friends. Why do so many story contents, video games deal with death and destruction on a large scale? Can a young brain deal with it cognitively or emotionally?

Attachment behaviour is crucial for normal emotional development of a young child. Cognitive development of a young child uses all the five senses to learn about environment, by looking, touching, listening, smelling and tasting, be it a ball or a biscuit. Screen time does not have scope for the above activities. It involves looking at a small screen and small finger movements of swiping. Once I gave a picture to a child to look at and she put her finger on the face in the picture and tried to zoom it. She did not understand that it was a real picture, or did not differentiate it from any onscreen picture.

Language development gets compromised by screen time. As the 30-million words experiment shows, children instinctively learn languages by interaction with others and by communication. Screen time cannot replace real talk. Exceptions are Skype, Face time and WhatsApp. But these are, thankfully, not accessible to primary school age children yet. If made accessible, they too should be accessed by kids within normal limits. Seeing a real flower or real face always allows more exploration and appreciation. If there is a chance for the real meeting, I would consider it the best option.

Language and Communication

Case 4

A case of aggressive behaviour in pre-school.

Recently, we had the parents of three-and-a-half years old Rajanish in our clinic. His teacher in the lower KG class had sent the referral, with complaints of ADHD and being aggressive with other children. What he said often was not understandable and disconnected. On occasions, he would repeat words he heard. The family had moved to Bangalore from Delhi two months earlier. In Delhi, in his play school, the teachers had noted some disruptive behaviour that the child continued to repeat in the new school.

On observation, we found him sitting on the chair, fairly composed, smiling, with the most charming expression on his face, though we were total strangers to him. When spoken to, he was alert and responsive. We discovered that he spoke only Hindi and we were not too good in that. We were told that he could play carom, Ludo and enjoyed jigsaw puzzles and colouring books. He would quietly do these activities up to 10-15 minutes without being restless. Nor did we note any restlessness during the entire session. *His aggressive behaviour was observed at school but not at home.*

He would fight if his elder sisters, who were much older than him, provoked him. He always helped the mother around the kitchen. He slept late in the night, at 11 pm, and had three hours nap in the afternoon.

He was very attentive when we talked to him and came up with lengthy replies. But when we diverted our attention to his parents, he would turn around in his chair and fidget a little. When we asked about screen time, they said he was very interested in TV and mobile programmes. He would pester his sisters and get them to use their mobiles. His father, noting his excessive interest, would put away his own mobile when Rajnish was around.

We asked him to show us how he plays the Ludo, and he showed us how he moved the various pieces and threw the dice very dramatically. Then he held up his arm and did an odd gesture of moving his wrist as if to pull something out of his shirt sleeves. We asked him what that was, as, for us, it was a movement unrelated to the dice. Then he said – that was how Spiderman initiates his actions! Obviously, the movement of the dice throwing, led him to the imagery of Spiderman's action. We also noted that he talked about Tom and Jerry action and Tik-Tok during his long conversation with us. It is then that we discovered that we could follow his 'stream of thoughts' only if we had the complete background of his screen time experience.

These are some 'possible strategies' that we suggested to help him:

i. Very limited screen time.
ii. Provide him with real activities, which he is very fond of at home and outdoors.
iii. When not engaged, he tended to fidget. As he enjoyed communication and was very sociable, we requested his teachers to seat him in a group of Hindi speaking children where he could engage in conversation. We felt, then he would get drawn into activities with these other children who spoke the same language.
iv. We found that the child dissociated himself from the immediate surroundings, when he was frustrated.
v. We suggested, his afternoon naps needed to be stopped because he needed to be in bed early as he needed to get up early for the school.
vi. He could come to our clinic for group sessions with young children with multiple disorders and languages.
vii. The child was very pro-social, communicative and very intelligent. These, we thought, would promote his recovery.

Perhaps, as clinicians we need to hone our diagnostic skills, knowing the difference in the background we were exposed to and the present-day children. The case reminded me of the insight offered long ago by Anna Freud – that like adults use Free Association (in their fantasy life), children use play to free associate. We need to understand that this is a form of communication as well.

Social Development

Especially for the very young, screen time does not promote pro-social behaviour.

Toddler learns about playmates and how to behave during play. A preschooler first indulges in 'solitary' play, where he is playing with a doll or building blocks. If another toddler comes in, he too uses the same space close by and plays. This is called 'parallel play' where the two will be looking at each other and play, but not together. The third stage is 'interactive' (cooperative) play, where they toss the ball to each other or build a fort with the building blocks together. This is when the toddler learns how to play cooperatively. Then this evolves into play with rules and 'fair play', which introduces both empathy and morality into play – leading to enhancement of pro-social behaviour.

There have been some classic experiments on children, recorded on videos and children mimicking the behaviour shown on the relevant video. A video shows a man tearing up a doll on the TV screen while a six-month-old child watches. In the next scene, an identical doll is given to the baby and he destroys the doll, exactly the same way as the man did in the earlier scene. This indicates that the child learns by imitation and this activates latent tendency to aggression. In addition, such aggression de-sensitises the pains of others, leading to lack of empathy. It also leads to acceptance of violence as the normal way of conflict resolution.

In Summary

(Adapted from the American Academy of Paediatrics)

- For children younger than 18 months, limit media use other than video-chatting.
- Do not feel pressured to introduce technology early; children will figure them out quickly, once they need to.

- For parents of children 18 to 24 months of age who want to introduce digital media, choose high-quality programming/apps and use them together (co-view) with children, because this is how toddlers learn best. Letting children use media by themselves should be avoided. Use only quality products – PBS Kids, Sesame Street may be permitted.
- In children older than two years, limit media to one hour or less per day of high-quality programming. Viewing together promotes enhanced learning, greater interaction, and limit setting. Help children understand what they are seeing and help them apply what they learn from the world around them.*

Parent-child interaction and unstructured social play are still useful in developing critical thinking and social skills which toddlers lack, including impulse control, emotional regulation, creativity, and task persistence.

Excessive TV watching at this age has been associated with cognitive, social, emotional and language delays. Additionally, excessive media use during pre-school years is associated with increased risk for obesity, possibly due to food-related advertisements, decreased physical activity and watching TV while eating/snacking, which, as we all know, makes for 'mindless overeating'. Excessive media use has been associated with decreased sleep even in infants, maybe from the screen's 'blue light' and the content watched.

---

* On 8 June 2020, the Indian State of Karnataka banned on online education by schools from pre-nursery to fifth grade, responding to opinions shared by child psychiatrists, and educational experts.
The decision applies to all schools within Karnataka regardless of their affiliation to central or State boards.
https://economictimes.indiatimes.com/industry/services/education/karnataka-bans-online-education-for-children-up-to-class-v/articleshow/76306008.cms?utm_source=contentofinterest&utm_medium=text&utm_campaign=cppst

Screen Time and Perilous Development

4 to 10 Years

THE SCIENTIST in the crib now moves on to the real world as an explorer. Piaget describes this stage where the logic is initially pre-operational and then ends with concrete operations. These are fixed stages of development of logic and vary across age, socio-economic slabs, culture and such other variables. But, on the whole, these are somewhat universal. The age of abstract reasoning follows as the final stage after the age of ten.

If child's understanding of what he sees and how he interprets it is of great importance at this age, in the earlier age of pre-schoolers, he may not understand what he sees, though he can mimic it. A six-year-old can actually misinterpret what he sees. His interpretation makes him happy or scared – though the event itself may be innocuous. Thus, it is important for parents to know what the content is and how it is being portrayed. *The parent should watch the programme instead of believing that all programmes are educational.* Special attention should be paid to commercials or advertisements. The content should be analysed and discussed with the child. Sometimes, even something innocuous can be addictive and replace reality.

Case 5

For example, my own grandson was addicted to *Thomas, the Tank Engine* and watched the show repeatedly. Once on a train journey in India, I pointed out to him at a major hub where we got out of the train and said, 'that train has a diesel engine'. He cowered with fear, 'Oh! No!'. I, as an adult, believed that he was interested in trains, coal, diesel or electric. But he was frightened because diesel was an 'aggressive and bad engine' in his show. Even simple narratives can have personalised qualities, which the child is made to believe in contrast to factual information about real trains.

This is about little Arun when he was five-year-old. His mother was expecting her second child and was depressed and ambivalent, though it was an expected pregnancy. Arun was left to his own devices to keep himself amused. He loved the Thomas Train series. Obvious, a favourite among many children of this age.

When the grandmother arrived to help out her daughter, she discovered Arun to be absorbed in watching Thomas endlessly. He refused to go out and play, would be restless and unable to play outdoors. The grandmother was alarmed by his obsession and intuitively decided a strategy to draw him out. Every evening, they would take him to the local railway station and watch the activities going on there for an hour or so. Though Arun was reluctant initially, his interest picked up as each day there were new adventures such as army battalion travelling, pilgrims travelling, hawkers selling things, different trains arriving and departing. Slowly, he began to experience greater joy at these expeditions to watch real trains and Thomas receded to the background. One day he came to the grandmother and said, 'Grandma, I don't know what was wrong with me! I was "possessed" by the TV. I could not stop myself watching Thomas. I am in control now. Now I can decide when I want to see TV and what programmes. But my mother too needs to learn to go off TV!'.

When offered the real fare, often children do try to kick the habit. This is a sample case of addiction where change of environment from TV trains to real trains can bring about a healthy change. Take for instance, advertisements about food and toys. There is an increase of eating of junk food in India. There have been decades of research on Maggi Noodles – the most favourite of junk food across the nation, across all social classes. Noodles made of plain wheat flour, embellished with monosodium glucomate to enhance the taste has overtaken the country's staple diets by storm. Now one sees that raagi, the most nutritious of the grains, is being replaced by the more expensive and not nutritious at all Maggi.

There is increased obesity in children in India, except in remote areas. But even then, Maggi noodles and white bread are considered delicious. Chocolates too are the best possible treats. The native diet across India often consisted of unpolished cereals, jaggery, coconut, fish, greens and so on. However, various food franchises have changed the diets of our children drastically due to their magical power of marketing.

Research Findings

In a dramatic vein Nicholas Karadaras (*Glow Kids: How Screen Addiction Is Hijacking Our Kids – and How to Break the Trance* 2016) describes how screens turn kids into psychotic 'junkies'. Many parents understand that the common glowing screens are having negative effect on children. Aggression and temper-tantrums are seen when taken away from the screens. The most tech-conscious parents such as in Silicon Valley, like Steve Jobs and others, are low tech in their own homes and send their own children to no-tech Montessori or Waldorf schools. The children hooked on to screen have wandering attention spans when they are not perpetually stimulated by the 'deliberately' hyper-arousing devices. In fact, they become bored, apathetic and uninterested when not plugged in.

Charles Wood et al (2019) studied the nature of agreement regarding the extent of screen time in 114 children of 9-11 years of age and adolescents and their parents and also studied the media use and health behaviour of the children. Both researchers in this study reported an hour each of video, apps and games, computer and the TV (a total of 4 hours) in almost similar reports. Disagreement occurred only when the child had his own TV in his room, where there was disagreement on hours of use. Adolescents reported 5 hours or more of screen time.*

Thus, it appears there is a fair extent of agreement on screen time in younger children and amongst adolescents, it becomes more complex.

This is an anecdotal account of a boy who 'wanted to be' a smart phone according to a newspaper report. The class teacher had assigned an essay about 'What I want to be' to the 4th graders. A ten-year-old boy wrote that he wanted to be a smart phone. The reasons given were as follows:

Both the parents, as soon as they came home from work, attended first to their mobiles. To paraphrase the essay, when the child wanted to talk to them about what happened at school or needed help with homework, they paid no attention. Even to play a game on the mobile, they preferred to play their own games and not with him. All these made him feel that they were more attached to their smart phones. They would love him, play with him and talk to him, if he were a smart phone. The boy's father saw his mother weeping and asked her the reason. She then told him the above story. The father asked who that boy was. She said, 'He is our son'. In fact, the mother – who was also the boy's class teacher – had given him the assignment.

iPhone Rivalry

While in my practice, sibling rivalries are often encountered but a new syndrome of 'iPhone rivalry' needs to be highlighted in the present case.

Anywhere, anytime, if two or more people meet, attending at once to the mobile than paying attention to the person/child in front of you is WRONG. *It means you are ignoring the person in front of you and it is demeaning to him or her.* There has to be a conscious effort to put away the techno-devices if you want to be a good parent and be a role model for your child.

Some Observations

- Screen time is passive and solitary activity.
- It affects children in different ways depending on age.
- What they know and experience is important.
- How much do they discuss with adults about what they understand?
- Drop in interest in academics and school is often seen.
- Reduced real time interaction with parents, siblings and friends is commonly encountered.
- Reduced interest in reading occurs as well.

There are times when parents use media to soothe a child, for example, during a plane flight or a doctor's office visit. That's not unreasonable and is sometimes necessary, but it is also important for children to learn how to regulate their emotions and soothe themselves. *Boredom is not a bad thing* and is known to stimulate creativity.

It's not just the kids. Parent's media use also decreases parent-child interactions and there are parents who use devices heavily and have kids who also do. The AAP recommends '... time limitations on digital media use for children 2 to 5 years old to no more than 1 hour per day, in order to allow children ample time to engage in activities important to their health and development and to establish media viewing habits associated with lower risk of obesity later in life. In addition, encouraging parents to change to educational and pro-social content and engage with their children around technology, which will allow children to reap the most benefit from what they view.'

In the preoperational stage of Piaget's theory of Cognitive Development:

a. The child is the centre of the universe. For example, a child may – while travelling in a car looking out of the window and seeing that the telephone/lamp poles, the trees or the moon is racing – believe that everything around him is moving without realising that it is he who is moving and not what he is seeing.
b. He also usually believes that two events occurring simultaneously are the cause and the effect.[3]

Case 6

One young boy in therapy with me once asked me if his grandfather was sick and dying, because he had kicked him, earlier on that day. The same boy had also reported that in their school, they were supposed to close their eyes, during morning school prayer. He discovered that the girl standing next to him had opened her eyes. So, he slapped her as she went against rules. This stage of the child is typically ego-centric and s/he has difficulty in understanding the other person's viewpoints or rights.

c. Another classic experiment is where a child is presented with a doll facing him by an adult and if asked whether the adult is viewing the back or the front of the doll, the child answers,'front' as he sees it – the front facing him.

3 For example, the famous Watson experiment at the core of behavioural approach was based on the event that a furry animal was presented to little Albert, accompanied by a fear-inducing loud gong. At this stage, children connect two unrelated events where they occur simultaneously.

Taking another person's perspective occurs in the next stage of cognitive development. In real life situations, children naturally learn that they are not the centre of the universe and learn to appreciate from the other person's viewpoints. Often, the adults around explain this as well.

Case 7

One overactive child while drawing on a large sheet of cardboard, with the idea of sharing and making three separate drawings with two other children, slapped the child who strayed into his area. That child in turn slapped him. He asked me in a puzzled way, why the other boy had slapped him. It is only when I explained that he had hit him first and what the other boy did was in response to it, that he understood. It was also explained to the other boy that he should have stayed within the area allotted to him. Children need to be made aware of the actions and the consequences of their behaviour.

These simple instructions are essential for the children in the pre-operational stage. By seven years, they grow out of this stage of logic. The pre-operational stage of logic is often puzzling to adults.

Now let us move on to what the TV/iPad/Video screens project. What would be their way of making children understand what the children need? Some good old-fashioned TV programmes did attempt story times which gave positive models for behaviour. But, at present, these are hard to come by. Even *Tom and Jerry*, one of the most popular cartoon series of the past decades, shows only aggressive content.

The idea that young children need finely calibrated contents of visual inputs while their stages of cognitive, emotional, social and language development is generally not considered necessary by the producers of the programmes. When children are immersed in their screen time, it is not possible for all the parents to judge the appropriateness of the content. So, they leave it to the wisdom of producers of the programmes and the advertisers. It is important to remember that children perceive differently at different ages. We need to be careful about their exposures, considering their age also.

Children in the different developmental stages and domains are uniquely different within themselves and compared to others in the same developmental stages as well as the ones that follow each other longitudinally. It is indeed a wonderful experience to get into this extraordinary phenomenon as some of the case studies reveal. The following are some examples, three are from my clinic. Here are the two incidents from the perspective of a grandmother:

Train Train Come Again

I am a grandmother of two boys, with a gap of 5 years 9 months between them, both exhibiting their own personality traits. Being with them I have learnt many things. I thought of sharing two incidents, involving each of them, in order to understand a child, his age and the effect of gadget on a child.

It was more than two years ago, when the elder one was six years old. I had watched 'The other pair', an Iranian short film on my mobile. The film was about a poor boy in the railway station mending his torn slippers, mesmerised watching another boy repeatedly wiping his pair of neat shoes he wore, sitting on the bench of the railway platform. Later the second boy had to get rid of his shoes and the first boy gets that pair. It is a nicely made film – of course, from the perspective of an adult. I showed it to my older grandson and waited for his responses. He was watching it silently, with his normal, peaceful expressions. He wanted to watch it again and did so for two more times. I was wondering what attracted him to it so much. I was feeling proud, considering his empathetic nature along with his emotional maturity.

I asked him to get clarity: 'What is it that you wished to see it so many times?' He plainly said, with an expression of wonder on his face, 'The bell rings each time before the train comes to the station!' I was mistaken, he was not interested in the two protagonists in the film.

I realised, we adults cannot be children. I was totally clueless that this simple ringing of the bell – that had no significance at all for me – could be what drew the child's attention. This is when I understood why the malice in cartoons is understood by adults at a very late stage. I also learnt that a child witnesses everything with the same freshness, which we adults cannot even imagine or consider foolish or insignificant.

While writing this incident, after more than two years, I wanted to reassure myself about his views. I showed the same film to the same child again. I was watching him, to get his responses very clearly. He watched it quite seriously and happily. When I asked him how the film was, his reply was, 'It was very nice!' I asked him what made it very nice for him. He said, 'The other boy gave his shoe away and the first boy got them both. It was very nice, that the boy got shoes for himself!' It was an unexpected response to my expectations. In the two years and a few month, the ringing of the bell and the coming of the train had lost its significance and the 'emotional' quotient was understood by the child.

When I had shown the film to the elder one for the second time, the younger one – of two years eight months age – had also come running and watched it. When the train arrived on the mobile screen, he began to scream excitedly and hurriedly – 'Grandma, the train, the train!!!' Yes, this was something I expected, because of my previous experience with the older child. He was jumping, hopping, dancing, singing. I did not heed much. But he was getting ready for something more exciting. His voice and actions (as he was not a fully articulate speaker yet) began increasing second by second. He finally communicated the wish that he wanted (as if we had waited for it and were supposed) to go in 'that' train, and began demanding that I – screaming and crying to tell me this – had to take him inside 'that' train. He, rather his age, was unable to understand or realise that we could not enter into 'that' train or that it was on screen, an image train, and was too small considering our sizes, etc., as we adults can think or do. When the train left the station (on the screen) he was helplessly screaming continuously – 'Grandma, the train went off, I had to go by it, you didn't take me, you didn't take me, please stop it and take me....'

By the end of the film, I saw two grandsons, one with a beaming serene smile and the other with an incessant flow of tears rolling down his eyes. The younger one was inconsolable for a very long time for not getting what he wanted.

A 4 minutes 35 seconds video (or a short film), that was considered a good one by an adult had such a varying impact on the same child during two different ages and two children of different ages. Age of the children, and their temperaments, exposures, backgrounds, and so many variables are there to invariably consider, to know the impact of what and how children view screen portrayals.

Contributed by KG Rajalakshmi

Case 8

A five-year-old had become very clingy with the mother and refused to part with her. At night too, he had to sleep between the parents. He did not want them to touch each other. In India, in many families, children sleeping with their parents is very common. On detailed interview it emerged that the child had seen the parents having sex. Subsequently, in a play session the child had revealed and re-enacted the same in what he thought was the father attacking the mother. In a very simple manner, the parents were asked to reassure the child that what he saw was not attacking. 'Daddy hurting the mother was like a tight hug, which you may mistake as hurting a person.'

Case 9

Yet another case is of Swathi, a ten-year-old girl, counseled and followed up by Vatsala Prasad. It was a very baffling case.

The girl was a bright, talkative, popular and happy-go-lucky child. She was very good in academics and extra-curricular activities. When her parents brought her for psychiatric consultation, they were most anxious about her. They said, 'Almost overnight, after a programme in school when she shared the stage with a group of girls, she suddenly started talking strangely'. When she saw a boy either nearby or on the TV, she said that she wanted to marry him. Thoughts of wanting to 'marry whomsoever' was the predominant theme in her mind. With us she was very friendly and communicative. She wanted to talk yet felt guilty and shy. She recalled the event which had precipitated the breakdown. She reported that after people left the auditorium, her best friend had slipped off her top and revealed her chest to a boy standing at the other end of the auditorium. Swathi was embarrassed and angry with her friend and had shouted at her and run off.

The girl had no history of sexual abuse. She had affectionate parents and one younger sister. Her over-talkativeness, irritability and continuous talking on erotic themes distressed her mother. She did not talk to the father about these things.

After several visits, her excessive talk and preoccupation continued in our presence, but she stopped such behaviour with the mother and in the school. When we suggested a second opinion, the psychiatrist thought it was ADHD and put her on medication. But she reacted badly to it, so the parents stopped it. Since she had become functional, we continued to see her as she still was symptomatic. She took the school exams and did very well as always and got several prizes in the extracurricular activities. My diagnosis was that it was an early manifestation of Affective Disorder. We kept a close eye on her for a year when she returned to normalcy at home and in school.

In one of her sessions with us, in an excited state, she once said that all the counsellors in our clinic were dressed up like Bharatanatyam dancers. During early months, when the mother reported remission and we still found her symptomatic with disturbed talk, I administered her the Rorschach Ink blot test.[4] She had a very quick reaction time, she became very frightened of the cards. She saw male and female genitalia, bleeding, pooping, peeing and disembodied fragments of human anatomy. If she had not responded in my presence, I would have diagnosed it as a case of most disintegrated schizophrenia in an adult.

Yet, the child also gave popular responses. Especially on the popular reality card with a butterfly or a bat. She said, 'That is a magical butterfly! Oh! No! It is not magical; it is crying in pain.'

'Why?' I asked.

'It is because it is giving birth, it is hurting and bleeding profusely.' She pushed the card away fearfully and anxiously as if it were real.

I asked her, 'Have you seen a child birth anytime?'

She said, 'Yes, it was scary!'

'Where and when?'

She said, 'On YouTube.' It was a revelation to me that we no longer are familiar with the real world of the children. I was out of my comfort zone as a child clinical psychologist. I needed to work on this book to remedy this lacuna in me as a clinician. It was a shock to me at my appalling ignorance of the tech-tsunami drowning our helpless children.

Anxiety and Confusion
Case 10

Nidhi is a 9-year old girl from an affluent family, staying in a village. She is from a joint family of 15 members. She was brought to our clinic with a complaint of masturbating and

4 A test that was developed by Hermann Rorschach, a Swiss psychiatrist. This is one of the earliest tests, used across the world, including India, to examine inaccessible and 'unconscious' mind. It consists of 10 cards with ink blots – five in black and white and the rest with colours – making no formal shapes or colours. Each one sees it differently, basing on one's familiarity in perception.

scratching her genitals, more so, when she was tense. The initial preparations / assumptions were towards any possible sexual abuse that might have occurred.

She was a shy child, of gentle appearance, speech and manners. The child did not give any clue of any physical harm done to her by anyone, in the family, outside or in school. When, once I had confirmed that nothing had happened at the physical level, I asked about her sibling.

She had a younger brother of one-and-a-half years and she was from a community where sons had a greater importance and were pampered. After extensive enquiry with the mother, sibling jealousy too was negated. Then I took up the issue of any gadget usage.

The mother said Nidhi was very fond of mobiles. She was almost a mobile addict. Then, after long questioning, the mother reported that she had once caught the child watching some sexual intercourse scene. The mother had taken away the mobile. Nothing was discussed or talked about, after that. Mobile usage continued, though. After that incident, the mother noticed the girl scratching her genitals, whenever stressed, like before examinations, whenever she was told some task, unpleasant for her to perform, etc. The mother was able to link these two aspects, only after being questioned in great detail by us. Left to themselves, the two aspects were totally independent of each other.

The child had come to us from a different place, during her summer holiday visit to her grandparents. We were unable to meet with the frequency required for the therapy to continue. So, I educated the mother on how to proceed with explaining sex to the child, peacefully, cautiously and carefully. She was told not to use mobiles, by reducing the usage hours, gradually.

Many scenes prompt or pop up on the mobile or any internet connected screen by themselves, to tempt and rouse the viewers' curiosity. When the users are children, naturally, being the massive bundles of curiosity, anything unexpected can happen. We have to be more aware of these intruders. And being adults, we may not understand what attracts a child. Each child, being unique , we cannot make a formula and bring out a manual as to the effects of these exposures on them, in general. They are vulnerable. So, we have to be more watchful, careful and conscious about the gadgets and their exposures.

Contributed by KG Rajalakshmi

In Britain, there have been effective ethical and moral guidelines set up by the government with television production companies and it is called the 'Duty of Care'. In 2009, concerns were raised over the programme, *Boys and Girls Alone*, which featured children aged 8 to 10 in a big-brother style reality show.

A review of the programme led to development of regulation which considered psychological risks to under 18s. These were multiple risks such as distress, trauma, negative attitude change, moral damage, lowered self-esteem, embarrassment, loss of dignity, disempowerment, insecurity, anxiety, engendered fears, mental stress, fatigue, peer disapproval or bullying (*The Psychologist*, July News, 2019).

We need such regulators in India also, not only for child reality shows but also for regular programmes on the various television channels as well as advertisements.

Some research findings that support the anecdotal accounts given above: Mental health professionals are alarmed at the widespread usage and impact of iPads, smart phones, Xboxes. Karadaras (2016) calls them 'digital heroin'. Schools too, promote their use.

According to the 2013 policy statement by the American Academy of Paediatrics, 8 to 10 years old spend 8 hours a day with various digital media, while teenagers spend 11 hours in front of the screens. Much of the research comes from South Korea, Japan and China. Aggressive temper tantrums and distractibility are commonly reported. There are some who become bored, apathetic and uninterested in everything when not plugged in or get into a trance-like state.

Donnely (2019), commenting on 'Duty of Care', has pointed out that Britain is 'medicalising' children instead of bringing them up properly, as the Head of the British Medical Sciences has warned. *Daily Telegraph* has launched a 'Duty of Care' complaint box, calling for more stringent regulation of social media sites, in order to protect children from harm. The need is to take action on underlying cases of the twin epidemics of obesity (related to advertisements for junk food) and mental health problem affecting today's children, the media house said.

In addition, advertisements and Instagram comparison of ideal beauty, causes the belief that one is ugly. An article in *Lancet* reported that children, who spent two hours a day on smart phones and video games, have significantly worse brain development than those with strict limits.

Some Vignettes

Mobile Hide and Seek

Case 11

Varshini is 10 years old. She loves watching videos on smart phone all the time. She has lost interest in any other activity or her schoolwork. She takes the phone into her bed, hides under the cover and watches videos all night long. Now-a-days she gets very impatient, angry and frustrated.

Contributed by Sujatha Reddy

My Gains versus Losses

Here is an anecdotal account, a rare retrospective self-report of how the child recognised the addiction herself.

In my own experience as a child, a brief stint with video games did me little good. When I was 6 years, I was given a *Super Nintendo* video game console which came pre-loaded with several games and the popular 'Duck Hunt'. This was a light gun zapper to shoot ducks that came on the screen. Of course, it involved quick reflexes and the ability to shoot down the creatures as they flew across the screen. I was thrilled with the hunting game and soon became addicted, often gobbling my dinner to go and shoot ducks.

I also became selfish and refused to share my game with other kids and playmates. Soon my mother realised the folly of giving me this form of entertainment and took it away. I was very angry and threw several tantrums, but my mother was firm and refused to let me play. Slowly, I got over this addiction and adjusted into other activities, spending more time reading and outdoors. When I look back, I remember my days with the video game sitting alone and playing with no social interaction with other kids. I gained little and, in the bargain, landed with eye strain and general restlessness.

My attention levels in all other activities took a beating as I always had the duck hunt at the back of my mind, thinking up strategies to shoot more ducks. I was restless and according to my mother, became very aggressive as somehow the use of the gun affected my self-image.

Contributed by Namitha Kumar

Free Play promotes physical and psychological wellbeing and creativity. Unlike virtual play, child-centred play allows the child to continue to be in touch with the surroundings. Orientation to one's own identity and that of others, time and place is of survival value. Virtual reality restricts the attention of the viewer only to the gadget.

---

* With the advent of Covid-19, online schooling has become the new normal. Children from Class 1 to Class 5 are normally subject to two hours every day of classrooms online.

Add to this three hours of some movie-or-the other time everyday, as playtime, park time, cycling time has been curtailed completely in most households.

Add to this about an hour of phone games time. Six hours every day has become the usual practice for most six-seven year olds in India.

Even poor children watch four-five hours of television and one hour of phone games, minus the online schooling. That is the reality of children in India under locked-down conditions.

Nature Needs Nurture in Adolescence

11 Years and Above

ADOLESCENCE IN Latin means to grow. It is linked to the onset of puberty. Puberty is characterised by bodily and physiological changes with a growth spurt. It is also associated with enhancement of domains of development in cognitive, language, emotional, social, moral and sexual spheres. There is a clear departure from childhood.

The adolescent brain development is at the peak level, only declining as s/he outgrows adolescence. He reaches the stage of the peak level of abstract reasoning, almost, adult level of maturity. He also matures psychologically and becomes independent in his relationships with family and grows closer to his peers. His identity as a person becomes strong. This may, at times, cause conflicts in the interpersonal relationships at home. This is often referred to as a 'generation gap'.

The generation gap as viewed by adults has been there for centuries. While generations have undergone changes, the complaints by adults about adolescents remain the same.

Adolescence is a critical but normal phase. It is considered a state of 'storm and stress', characterised by emotional turmoil, but not all adolescents necessarily go through it. It is a state where specific mental health problems such as lack of interest in schools, indulging in gang activities, drug/alcohol and internet abuse may surface. Enhanced sexual awareness and preoccupations and gender identity may arise.

India is a young country. In India, 10 to 19 years are considered as adolescents. Here, 15 to 24 years are considered youth. Every 5th person in the country is an adolescent. Every 3rd person is young. As much as 41 per cent of the people are below 20 years of age. During adolescence, up to the age of 10 years, boys and girls grow at the same rates. Between 10 to 12 years, girls grow faster. Between 12 to 18 years, boys have their growth spurt. Between 11 and 13 years most children enter puberty. In the wealthier nations and social classes, girls attain puberty earlier, compared to underprivileged girls with malnutrition.

Adolescents have some common problems during this period. Individual adolescents have issues such as privacy, family relations. Early problems can be in terms of discipline, relation to siblings, feeling victimised, hypercriticism, immaturity, rebellion against adults and lack of supervision, self-esteem, guilt and change in circumstances.

Confidentiality: In India, it is an alien concept.

With most people living in physical or psychological joint families, there were no secrets between the members. Everything had to be out in the open.

Then flew in the idea of confidentiality, especially in the upper class, a Western concept especially in the life of adolescents. They now do not accept anyone examining their personal diaries, mobiles and in fact even their rooms. The parents whom I meet often, however, continue to believe that they are entitled to know everything about the child. Thus, they have a curious ambivalence to the idea that adolescents need privacy. This takes a serious turn when it comes to screen time addictions. Family relations may have been a smooth ride, most children being obedient to parents when younger. At adolescence, the children seek out peers and become less accountable to the parents. This leads to common conflicts leading to fights, mistrust and anger outbursts between parents and the teenagers. I have met a good number of parents who fight with their teenagers as if they are still small children and do not deserve any respect as individuals. Parents often refuse to accept that their children are grown-up now. They also resent their close relationships with boys and girls unknown to them.

Self-Esteem: In adolescence it is a fragile trait. Their identity and self-esteem get bruised easily. Harsh and negative comments and physical punishments (which parents and teachers freely administer in India) bruise the self-esteem of the teenagers. One must treat teenagers with respect and not physically punish them. If the parents do not stop it, sooner or later they will be hit in return. Exposure to aggression at home can get aggravated by exposure to screen time aggression.

Guilt: Teenagers are more at risk for feelings of guilt, in their negative interactions with parents, siblings and friends.

Depression associated with guilt can make the teenager ruminate on suicide as a solution to all problems. In India, the parents invest a lot of money, emotions related to prestige and make topping or passing examinations as the most cherished value. When a teenager falls short of those ambitious expectations of the parents that he has internalised, there are instances of suicides attempted or completed among teenagers. Rumination about suicide is common in this age group and also the know-how to go about it. There was a recent newspaper account of largescale mix up in the announcement of exam failures, resulting in suicides of several youngsters. Perhaps parents should know that there is more to life than academic success. Hence there should be no academic pressure.

There is also additional stress of coaching classes, where it is 24/7 pressure to study. For example, 'Kota, a Coaching Town' in Rajasthan is reputed to bring in excellent results. There are several reports of severe stress resulting in suicides in this resident population of scholars, living there with the sole purpose of passing exams with flying colours. There are some other problems which adolescents as a group face. These are study problems, social withdrawal, peer problems and absenteeism.

Study Problems: Indian education system is **teacher-centric** and is based on rote learning. Consequently, apart from classroom lessons, students are forced to take additional tuitions, coaching classes, use guidebooks, faulty, shoddily and inaccurately prepared simplified textbooks that are easy to memorise. All the above are antitheses of 'empowered pupil-centred learning'.

However, globally, it is individual creativity and imagination and activity-based programmes that are recommended to be adopted.

These days, there is also the concept of uses of lesson applications. For example, there are techno-schools which children enter with built-in internet facilities, which promise to turnout IT professionals. In fact, two of the 16-years old visiting our centre last year were from two different techno-schools. They were in our centre as they were both screen time junkies and were out of school and aggressive with parents.

One girl, on admission, went into depression and recovered upon rejoining her old school. In fact, in the USA and Australia, such schools are being shut down due to the adverse effects on the mental health of youngsters. Use of more applications does not necessarily assure quality of education in real time.

Social Withdrawal: Adolescence can be a socially awkward age. Many children become withdrawn due to anxiety or depression. They may also withdraw due to bullying or isolation by the peers. They might also become victims of screen addiction, living in the world of fantasy, with gaming and social media friends. In fact, criticism on social media may aggravate depression.

Acting Out: Oppositional behaviour at home and in school too is a common manifestation. These can be aggravated by aggressive gang members. Individual and group acting-out behaviour may occur.

Absenteeism: Truancy or absenting oneself from school may occur in some children. Reasons are many. Conduct disorder, lack of interest in completing class assignments, non-completion of homework, bullying, disciplinary action for disruptive behaviour and so on. Sometimes, parents may not be aware that the teenager is not in school as he leaves and returns home at the regular time as most children do. In fact, there are known cases where they have been absent for 3 to 4 months in the extreme cases. But in most cases, it would be few weeks to few months. Usually, it is the school that notifies the parents. *School absenteeism is a serious mental health and social problem and needs to be urgently attended to.*

Peer Problems: These are very common among the teenagers. They may not feel that they belong to a group they identify with. It could be that even a small number of friends one likes to align with, refuse to take them in. These events create great deal of stress as peer group acceptance is essential. Shunning, humiliation or bullying can cause trauma to the victim.

On the other hand, one can be part of a group of bullies or aggressive youngsters. This group is at risk for indulging in criminal activities or drug/alcohol addiction. Internet bullying is a very common phenomenon. *Blackmails, sexting, stalking can all be part of the internet bullying.*

Change of Circumstances: Circumstances such as breakdown of the marriage of parents, being separated from the close-knit joint family, being sent to hostel (viewed as a punishment), change of home, school, teachers and group of friends too can be stressful. One such example, if one has excelled in a small school from a small town, is when a child is moved to a large anonymous school, it can be stressful especially when there is a change of medium of instruction from a regional language to English.

Need for an Inclusive Approach to Adolescence

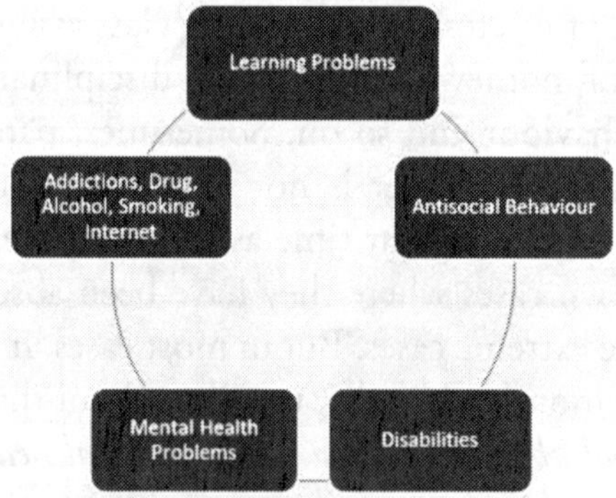

Reduce the impacts of the above

Enhance positive aspects of empathy, morality and prosocial behaviour

An adolescent's life is complicated by learning problems, poverty, antisocial behaviour, mental health problems, addictions to tobacco, drug, alcohol and internet and family disabilities including the ability to empower a child, send him to school and social exclusion. The impact of the above need to be reduced by attending to those together or individually in individual or group counselling.

There is a need to enhance positive aspects, healthy overall development by enhancing empathy, morality and prosocial behaviour.

Most Important: these values are to be inculcated in real time and not in a virtual world. In fact, as most of the content on internet focus on negative and unhealthy thoughts or behaviours, they are titillating as well as easy to identify with to the teenagers.

Myths about Benefits of IoT and AI

These are promoted by Amazon, Apple, Google and Microsoft and advertising and marketing agencies.

Most educated and well-to-do parents are persuaded in India and abroad to believe that technology allows them to be closer to children, than their own families when they were growing up.

Several research studies have indicated this perception of the parents that are really contrary to reality. The reality of a gadget-driven home is that everyone in the family walks into the house, immersed in their devices. It is a house, not a 'home'. There is no personal interaction here, there is only interaction with a device. The gadget-fascination spills into the outside as well.

When you go in the Metro or a Bus, you will find teenagers, while sitting or standing together, do not talk or look at each other. When they interact, they show each other their mobiles. Be it a dinner out, a wedding reception or even a music concert, youngsters are immersed in the visual treat on the mobiles instead of what is in front of them. Mostly, entire events are recorded directly or via selfies without the teenager looking at real event.

I recall with astonishment my visit to a magnificent temple near Dharamshala in Himachal Pradesh. The entire temple complex was slanted, perhaps due to frequent earthquakes in the area. A couple of teenage tourists, indeed international ones, were immersed in their iPads. They were not even aware that they were around a breath-taking beauty – a 10th century temple ruin. Travel is supposed to widen your horizons, while tech devices keep you from learning everything about the ever changing and fascinating world around. The screen shows you repeatedly the same thing.

Is one sunrise same as another? Video gaming is meant to be addictive as it is meant to enable the tech giants to acquire ever-increasing wealth.

Some Research Findings

Doing technology research on the 'wired' young, researchers Gustavo Mensch and Illan Talamud (2013) sum up their findings thus: Most of the empirical evidence on association between internet use and family time shows a reduction in the time parents and youth spend together.

A study published in Archives of *Paediatrics and Adolescent Medicine*, reports that, teens who spend more time playing on computer (not on homework) or watching TV were less attached to parents than those who spend relatively less time with the screens. Online gaming hurt teen's relationship with parents. A Korean study of 4th to 6th graders shows that online gaming decreases family time, while homework does not. Unfortunately, kids tend to use internet and computers for entertainment as they spend only 10 minutes doing homework or gathering educational information online.

Parents' use of technology too affects the family. Parents may communicate via technology, but if that exceeds face to face interaction among the family, it is counter-productive.

A Stanford University study shows that an hour an adult spends at home on the internet reduces the family 'face time' by 24 minutes. The researchers use the Annenberg school personal interactive technologies' questionnaire to report that there was significant decrease in 'relational distances' among parents and their 12 years old children in the years from 2005 to 2008. I wonder why actual interaction between children and parents in terms of actual talking, singing, playing or reading has to be taken over by internet instead of the normal and routine activities.

Michael Gilbert of Stanford warns that, 'Family breakdown leads to obstructive behaviour'. Catharine Steiner Adair (2006-2008) of Harvard Medical School interviewed more than 1,000 children, 500 parents and 500 teachers, described the result of her study as 'a big disconnect between parents and children' though they appeared to be connected by being wired.

Brains are endowed with high plasticity, as Daniel, Siegal and Mary Hartzell (2011) say: 'Experience shapes brain structure. Experience is biology. – How we treat our children changes who they are and how they will develop. Their brains need a parental involvement. Nature needs nurture.' This includes all the caregivers, not just the parents.

(i) Kids with healthy **parent attachment** regulate their emotions better, score higher intellectually, have higher self-esteem than those with no such bond. In adolescence, they are less likely to be depressed. They receive better grades and fewer behaviour problems. They are also less likely to abuse drugs or alcohol.

(ii) **Consequences of life with digital machines:** A Kaiser Foundation study shows that heavy media users are likely to get into trouble, suffer distress and are often bored. They are also susceptible to cyber bullying.

Importance of Self-Control for Children

The Marshmallow test: Walter Michel, a Psychology Professor at Columbia University since 1960s, has studied the self-control of four years old by an ingenious test called the Marshmallow (a sugary sweet) Test. Four year old children were given the options of eating the sweet on a table as soon as the child sees them or wait for 15 minutes. If the child does not eat the first one for 15 minutes, the child will be rewarded with an additional sweet. This experiment rewards 'self-control'. When these children reached adulthood, children who had experienced self-control in delayed gratification generally had higher self-control and performed academically better. A simple test, yet with such predictive power. It proves that self-control indeed is very important.

A New Zealand study (Mohitt et al) followed subjects from birth and found those with self-control at 3 to 5 years performed better in all domains throughout and were less likely to do drugs or alcohol, commit crime or have financial problems. Most importantly, the message is that self-control can be improved.

A Pennsylvanian University study result says that the teens with self-control spent more time with homework and got higher grades. *It is claimed that self-control is twice as important as intelligence. Self-control is the most vital component in health handling of the digital world.*

In a poor country like India, where majority of school children are in government schools, year-on-year, for the last decade, it is being reported that seventh graders have reading, writing, maths skills of second graders. When there is paucity of infrastructure, shortage of teachers, school full of disadvantaged children, can we afford fancy tech gadgets? What should be the priority of infrastructure providers, is a question well asked.

At the same time, we must take note that, even the poorest illiterates in India have mobile phones. It is a necessity to conduct not only small businesses but keeps the service sector going. It also ensures parents at work are able to communicate with their children, old people are able to remain in touch and migrant workers can be in touch with their distant families. In today's India, a mobile is a cost-cutting, empowering device. In a situation of total lockdown, a mobile phone has proved its need time and again. There is no way today to argue against Digital devices. Westerners can be educated in safeguarding their children. How do we reach out to our poor parents who are in the awe of their tech-wizard offspring? The only way forward is to make them aware of the demon lurking in the devices.

Every parent needs to be explained at length, as long as the mobiles are used in talking to the family or friends or for keeping in touch, they are very useful. But playing game or being on social media can be too addictive. Time spent on an electronic device, be it a smartphone or the television, should be monitored by the parents and teachers. The time spent on it should be within limits, set voluntarily by the children themselves in cooperation with teachers and parents. It should not take over play time or school time. It should not be more than a total of three hours in a day, divided between morning and evening.

Let us also be realistic in our enthusiasm to promote tech education in a poor country like ours. It is the corporate houses that acts as 'Do Gooders', often funding technology in poor schools. Expensive flash cards or iPads are seen as 'manna' from the heaven by the teachers and parents of the 'have not' children. Let the corporate houses confine their doles to food, uniforms, books for the 'natural and real children', school buildings, playgrounds and toilets and not introduce underprivileged kids to gadgets before they are in high school.

Adolescence and Screen Time

Adolescence is a critical natural phase of sensation seeking. But, impulsivity regulation, in other words 'self-control', is required. The buzz word for them is **heavy on accelerator – light on brakes.** This needs to be changed to **Light on accelerator and heavy on brakes**. There are myths that (a) adolescents need peers more than parents and (b) interactive screen time can replace real friends. This is simply not true and is marketed by mythmakers in the industry.

Parents are needed to be unconditionally supportive and love the teenagers yet SET LIMITS to all behaviours including their relationship with tech gadgets. In fact, being only with peers and not with parents increases delinquency, drug/alcohol and interactive screen time addictions. Contrary to the common belief, adolescent stress is **increased** with **peers** and causes decreased attachment and amplified frictions with supportive parents.

My Own Battle Ground

Case 12

Prasad, a 15-years old boy, came to the Child Guidance Clinic (CGC), with his parents complaining of PUBG (Player Unknown's Battle Ground, a game) addiction. He was also very active on social media like Facebook and was on it most of the time. He said that he could not go on without checking his WhatsApp or playing PUBG for a long time. This had affected his academic performance and also made him increasingly angry with his parents as they kept nagging him about his phone usage.

He said that if his parents let him play on the phone, then it meant that they loved him. Another of his complaint against his parents was that they did not buy him a high-end smart phone when all his friends had their own high-end smart phones. Not having a high-end smart phone made him feel inferior in his peer group. This had also led to outbursts of anger.

Contributed by Sujatha Reddy

Phone, Phone You Are Mine!

Case 13

Sankalp was 19 years old and studying in 2nd year of college when he came for counselling. He had scored an aggregate of 73 per cent in his 10th board exams and 85 per cent in science subjects. He is on his phone all the time and unable to stop using his smart phone. He failed in one subject in his 1st year in college and so had to change the college. In 2nd year of college, he failed in 4 subjects. He was angry at parents because they were blaming his phone usage habits for his academic failure.

Contributed by Sujatha Reddy

Case 14

Subbu was 14 years of age, studying in 9th standard, when he was brought in by his mother and older cousin with the complaints of computer game addiction, self-harm and running away from home for two days in the second week of March 2018.

Subbu lived with his parents who ran a saree store from their home. Both the parents traveled to procure the sarees and when in Bangalore, they were busy running their shop. His father was 57 years of age and had no formal education. His mother was 38 years old and had attended school till 8th standard. Subbu had two older sisters, the elder studying BSc. and the younger sister in 2nd year of engineering. Both the sisters were busy with their studies.

Subbu's primary caregiver was his grandmother who lived with them. She was a simple lady who loved her grandson and she did not understand the uses of computer and technology. She had no formal education and believed that if her grandson could use a computer; he was really very intelligent.

When Subbu was 9 years old, a computer café opened near their house. Subbu would ask his grandmother for money to go and play on the computer. She felt that it was a better option for her grandson to play on the computer than getting involved with boys in their neighbourhood, as that would need more monitoring. If he was in the computer café, she need not worry. So, whenever Subbu wanted to play, she would give him the money.

After his grandmother passed away, he started pestering his mother to give him the money to play. He would get extremely angry, disobedient till his demands were met. He would lie to his mother and teachers. Subbu played a game called 'Dota 2'. It is a multiplayer online battle arena videogame. The game holds multiple battles and competitions. Subbu wanted to skip school to play the game.

After four years, when Subbu turned 13, his parents saw his academic performance take a huge plunge and decided to shift him to a residential school. His performance did not improve. Then he got bullied and refused to continue in the residential school. When they brought him back home next year and enrolled him to a school nearby, he would not submit his test papers. He refused to go to school and when the teacher asked him to bring his parents to school, he ran away from home.

He was gone for two days, slept at a park near the house and came back home on the third day. When he was asked why he ran away, he said that they – his family – would not let him play the games. He would pick fights with his sisters and pester them to give him their computers so he could play games online.

During the counselling session, when he was asked what he thought of his family, he said that they were trying to protect him from wasting time and they did it because they loved him. He said, when he wanted to play on the computer, he could not think and he just wanted to play. He did not like to miss the tournament and other events in his game.

When he was asked what he wanted to do in the future when he grew up, he replied that when aliens come to attack the earth, he would be ready to fight with them. It appeared that he had moved into his virtual world and believed that it was the reality.

Subbu was referred to the Technology de-addiction centre in NIMHANS, Bangalore. When I called his mother one year later, she mentioned that he went for 2 sessions and then dropped out. She said that he had reduced his game playing to 1 hour a day.

Contributed by Anitha Sudhir

Growing up with TV

Case 15

Pratham was a 15-year old boy studying in 10th standard, living in a nuclear family. He was the only child. He was exposed to screen time since he was an infant.

The television was on all the time in his house. Father had a long working day and the mother did not know how to speak or interact with the child. The mother was always glued to the

TV and so was the child. Two uncles stayed with the family till Pratham was about 6 years old and they could play with the child only for few hours in the evening, after their working hours. Most of the family members were addicted to TV.

At the age of three years, a desktop PC also arrived at home. In the name of introducing rhymes to the child, computer also came into use for full time. Later, when the child was around 5, he learnt to play games on the computer.

Then his home was upgraded with laptop, tab and mobiles. Now the child had access to gadgets, wherever he went. At the age of five years, the child was able to name all the TV serials which played on TV since morning to night in a perfect order, with all the characters in most of the serials.

Effects of Too Much Screen Time in Pratham – How it Evolved:

As a child, there was delayed speech. Pratham could speak only two words at the age of 3 years and sentences only at around 5 years of age. Even today, his speech is unclear. He speaks very fast and misses words also in between.

He sleeps very little as he keeps on playing mobile games till late into the night and starts playing as soon as he wakes up, even without performing his daily routine.

He eats too much and does not know what he eats.

He wets his bed in sleep and goes to the toilet once in 3 or 4 days.

He is poor in socialisation. He speaks very little even with the first circle of his family members. He is attached to only one uncle, who stayed at home when he was a child and that too, as he buys the latest phones.

He is poor in academics.

Contributed by Arathi Rao

How to Enter the Real World without Insight?

Internet addiction is becoming a severe problem amongst many adolescents. They are more vulnerable to internet addiction, as they have less ability to control their enthusiasm for internet activities.

Case 16

A 14-year old adolescent girl presented herself, along with her mother at our centre. The mother complained that her daughter was aggressive, agitated and had compulsive behaviour. In the last two years, her academic performance had also come down.

The girl was developmentally a normal adolescent. Her parents were from a middle-class family. Her father was working for a company in Malaysia and mother was Yoga Therapist in Bangalore.

In a couple of sessions, it was confirmed that, besides schooling, she avoided all other activities. She had no friends in the neighborhood and hardly interacted with family members. She enjoyed being alone. Her companion was the phone/TV.

During vacation she never went out anywhere but sat at home, daily on mobile or television for nearly 8 to 10 hours. Whenever her mother asked her to stop viewing after 2 hours (time limit given) she said, 'just 5 minutes' which would never come. Forcibly, when she was stopped from watching TV, she threw tantrums – threw things and hit people or went and locked herself in a room. Her appetite was poor and she slept only for 4 to 5 hours.

The first step in treatment was the recognition that a problem exists.

The child has not understood and seems to be comfortable with the internet for hours together, though it hindered her normal life. She has no insight.

First, the mother is being counselled for self-awareness and to change her parenting style.

Contributed by Sheela Kamath

Warning Sign:
DANGER-Technology Speeds Up Detachment

Child Development, Mental Health and Diversities

CHILD AND adolescents' overall development, mental health and disabilities and diversities form a wide canvas on which globalisation casts its imprint.

To understand and promote overall development of children in India, we need to delve into the diversities that keep India united as well as divided over the centuries. It is most essential in the background of technical globalisation. As a rule, these technology benefits do not reach Indian population groups, which are diverse, divided by multiple languages, religions, socio-economic classes, education, disabilities and cultures, easily. Access to technology is a Have and Have Not issue in India. Technology access can empower as well as doom people. Any 'solution for all' model can be simplistic.

Now that the Genie of IoT and AI is out of the bottle, how do we deal with it?

TEMPLATE-PSYCHOPATHOLOGY IN THE CONTEXT OF DEVELOPMENT

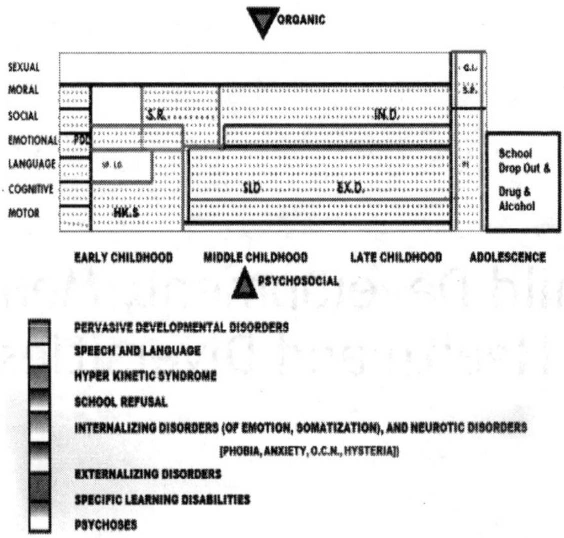

Mental Health Concerns

There are two groups of developmental disorders. These mostly start very early and soon after birth. They are pervasive in nature, almost influencing and mostly comprising all the domains of development. These are physical, intellectual, language, emotional, social, moral and sexual development. When most of all the domains are compromised, these are considered as pervasive developmental disorders. The major categories are disabilities where intellectual, visual, hearing, language and motor movements are compromised. The disabilities are listed under 10 categories including minor ones.

The other major category is Autism Spectrum Disorders (ASD). Here, we are looking at Developmental Disorders and ASD, with this diagnosis from very early childhood onwards, with focus on rehabilitation, remediation or training with intense efforts.

Autism Spectrum Disorders (ASD) and Disabilities are characterised by visual, speech, hearing, motor, cerebral and the main ones are pervasive developmental disorders and more debilitating disorders under this category. ASD is characterised by social withdrawal, difficulty in emotional bonding, and deviant language and communication.

Specific Developmental Problems and Disorders

The examples of these are poor motor coordination, delays and disorders of speech and language, daytime and bedtime wetting (enuresis) or soiling (encopresis) along with Specific Learning Disorders. All the above problems start at very young age.

Attention Deficit and Hyperactivity Disorder (ADHD)

This is characterised by overactivity, impulsivity and attention deficit. It begins at around the time the child starts to walk. Instead of walking, he runs and climbs. He is highly distractible and often very impulsive. However, the symptoms may be present all the time in all situations and is called **pervasive** hyperactivity. It is also known that some children have only **situational** hyperactivity. One preschooler is overactive and difficult to manage not only at home but also in preschool. Another child may be very docile and obedient at home (especially where parents are very strict and punitive) but in school he is very difficult to manage, with the friendly teachers. Situational hyperactivity need not be diagnosed as true ADHD. By changing the caretaking styles and the environment, the child may become normal. But if it is pervasive in all the contexts, the child needs to be treated for ADHD.

Is ADHD a product of new age civilisation?

This is a very controversial issue. Renowned psychologists like Jerome Kagan have questioned the very existence of this construct, and say it owes much of its popularity due to the pharmacology industry. Examples being in the USA, where a very large number of children are being diagnosed as ADHD and put on anti-stimulants and maintained on it for long periods. This puts them at risk for drug abuse as teenagers.

In the UK and in India, the guideline for stimulant use is stricter and used as last resort. We should first try psycho-social measures of remediation, behavioural approach and so on. These seem to work well on a good number of children. The WHO 11, of course, has this diagnostic category as epidemiological surveys in the West and in India (mostly urban) have shown somewhat similar prevalence.

Nature & History of Diagnosis of ADHD

Both, the International Diagnostic Systems DSM-5 and the ICD-11 categorise ADHD as a disorder. In addition, there is mounting evidence that screen time is related to the incidence of ADHD.

Jerome Kagan has influenced the study and treatment of ADHD. Kagan's work centred on *mind of the child,* yet brain too was important and the two interact constantly. Kagan gave a unique interpretation of emotion. He described in four phases: A brain state is caused by an incentive, changes in the body movement, body feelings and in the facial expressions along with muscle tension. One of his major contribution has been his study of temperament. There were two groups of infants. Those who get startled easily and move to new things and those who remain calm.

In his study, the highly reactive infants grew up into shy and anxious children while those with low reactivity grew up as calm children. Kagan believes that there is over-diagnosis of mental illness in children. In earlier times, *misbehaviour or failure to excel were explained as natural to childhood.* They were held accountable for their actions and assumed to be normal kids.

Kagan believes that ADHD does not exist. He believes that the diagnosis is an invention and not a real condition. According to him the diagnosis is promoted by pharmaceutical industry as 90 per cent of these children diagnosed are put on medication; he thinks they do not have abnormal dopamine metabolism. If drugs are available, the doctors will make a corresponding diagnosis.

Kagan is considered the more impactful psychologist than Carl Jung and Ivan Pavlov, so one cannot simply dismiss his ideas. I had the privilege of meeting him in person at Harvard. He was one of the most impressive, kind and compassionate persons I have met. I discussed with him my belief in the diagnosis of reactive autism, having failed in convincing my colleagues. He was supportive of my views, about the possibility of psychological origins of autism.

Kagan is scathing in his criticism of the pharmaceutical industry. The excessive amount of money circulating from the sale of drugs is creating a number of problems, he says. There is collusion among the industry, politicians and the doctors. Take for example, the current epidemic of opioids among youth. Following stringent regulations, the crisis is waning. The profit loop consists of the physicians who benefit from prescribing depressants to ADHD. Big pharma spends lot of money on politicians. Parents are convinced that the child has ADHD. Thus, ADHD is both misdiagnosed and over-diagnosed.

Have we a right to administer mind altering drugs to children?

Dr Victoria Denkley, a child psychologist, after studying numerous disorders such as ADHD, oppositional deficit behaviour, sleep disorders, mood disorders explored and found an underlying syndrome and boldly called it the 'electric screen syndrome'. She found that the number of kids diagnosed with bipolar disorder had increased 40-fold between 1994 and 2000. Between 1998 and 2007, the diagnosis of ADHD had increased 800 per cent. She speculates that electronic screen wreaks havoc on still-developing nervous system, making it 'wired and tired' and she has recommended 'tech fasts'.

However, my own work in the tribal areas in South India offers a stark contrast. Of the 800 tribal primary school children, who lived in residential facilities (Ashram Schools) run by the Social Welfare sector of the Government of India, I have not found a single case of ADHD.

This set me thinking as in our own Child Guidance Clinics in urban areas, a good number of ADHD children come and qualify for the diagnosis. But in one study in schools – of the 100 children diagnosed by teachers (on Connors test) as ADHD, only 10 received clinical diagnosis in our clinic. This meant that *teachers were over-diagnosing ADHD*. A good number of normal children are overactive in childhood and overactivity wears off as the child gets older. Why was there no ADHD cases in my tribal project area?

Behaviour observation revealed that all the children from class 1 to 7 in the residential facility showed remarkable pro-social behaviour. As these hostels had very few staff except a cook and a teacher, older children helped the younger ones in braiding hair, getting ready in the morning and so on. They acted as older siblings.

All children initially were very shy and fearful of us, but as part of the project, we took them school supplies, art, craft and play material. We also encouraged storytelling, dances, proverbs and riddles in their mother tongues. Our programme of child-centred play was immensely popular and they loved our visits. They would ask if we had eaten our meals, would we like to share their meals and so on. In contrast to the free art drawings of urban primary school children, they drew many adults and children holding hands (like a human chain) describing it as 'me, siblings, parents, grandparents, cousins, aunts and uncles'. It was such a delightful expression to the community feeling they shared.

Around the time of my research, there was no electricity in the tribal colonies. The hostels were dark and dingy. Children studied outdoors or wherever there was ventilation and light. Most significant was that there were no movie houses, TV or mobiles. Even today, you can find such villages. This set me thinking, ADHD is a product of the modern civilisation and its artefacts. My project area is in the Nagarahole Wildlife Reserve of South India. Elephants were frequently seen raiding crops or wandering into the school yards in the evenings. So, schools closes by 3 pm so that the teachers can get home safe. The forest range is open to traffic only between 6 am and 6 pm. Children spend their entire day amidst the rich flora and fauna of these rain forests.

It is in big urban schools that we find mental health problems including ADHD in children. It is generally believed that 'ADHD is a Nature Deficit Disorder'.

The Big Questions

What causes ADHD? Or specifically is screen time one of the causes of ADHD?

J Gamino suggests the following:

1. Brain imaging research shows the frontal cortex controls impulsivity (a key component of ADHD) and it gets compromised by excessive screen stimulation. Wang et al (2011) compared gamers and non-gamers and found less activation in the brain regions after 10 hours of videogame playing for one week and that this was instrumental in impulsivity and emotion regulation.
2. On the other hand, clinically one finds dramatic decrease in the symptoms when the screen time is completely cut or drastically reduced. This is common even in my clinical experience.

Has Internet Gaming Disorder (IGD) moved from being a recreational activity to something causing or resulting in a serious psychotic disorder as it comes under the DSM-5 classification?

A study of association between a psychiatric disorder termed Hikikomori (reclusive behaviour of psychotic proportions) and Internet Gaming Disorder was carried out by Starvopoulos et al (2019). The IGD study consisted of players playing online (what is known as a massively multiplayer online game). As many as 153 Australian youth and 467 North American youth were assessed on short scales to measure both IGD and Hikikomori syndrome. The study reported strong association between the two and the only difference was that the Australian patients stayed with their parents. Whether family supports are helpful or not is yet to be studied.

There is one in-depth qualitative study of the inner world of gamers by Jing Si et al (2019). In this case, 16 problem gamers were studied across 5 countries. The study indicates that:

i. Gaming was reported to be a meaningful and purposeful activity consisting of both positive and negative experiences.

ii. The individual, interpersonal and environmental influences simultaneously exert pull and push influences, which determines the amount of gaming.

iii. Intervention could include 'minimising' pulling and training to 'push' towards desired activities.

The traditional notion of social activity has changed. With the advent of social media, games began as recreation, but no longer remain so. The progammers actually view ABT Bill-700 (an Anti-c-Met Monoclonal Antibody) generated in humans under certain special conditions as a method of coping with stress!

In India

In a study by a psychiatrist among Indian ascetics, RL Kapur describes it as 'their ways' and as 'Another Way to Live'. A collaborator and observer, this author recalls that the reclusive psychotics became revered inmates of the ashrams, being taken care of completely while no demands were made on them. Indian ashrams in the Himalayan regions offer traditional hospitality to the homeless and people on the fringe. They are not labeled, only supported and offered a sanctuary in the true sense of the term during their lifetime.

In the Western world, however, people who are shy and asocial, may find gaming as the only safe refuge.

This is to suggest gaming too may provide security to people who are misfits in any society, with the proviso that their aggression should not be allowed to manifest as violence against self or society.

Disorders of Emotion and Conduct

In other words, in the American parlance, these are Internalising and Externalising disorders.

In the Internalising disorders, the child is mostly sad, quiet, withdrawn, fearful, anxious and shy. If present very early in childhood, this could be the temperament of being 'slow to warm'. If there is an onset of the Hikikomori syndrome or IGD, there should be a precipitating factor. The same features, if they continue to adolescence, may be termed anxiety or depression, and it may be considered a disorder.

Externalising disorder consists of disruptive and aggressive behaviour. Aggression may be verbal or physical. Bullying, stealing, lying may also be present. Disobedience and oppositional behaviours are common. There may be a continuity of ADHD features later on, present with externalising disorders. During adolescence, both internalising and externalising behaviour may get aggravated.

Depression and anxiety in Adolescence Clinical Research on Increased Internet use and Depression:

Table 1 Web Use and Mental Health

1998 Carnegie Mellon study web use over two years	Showed depression
2012 Missouri State University 30% 2/6	Showed depression
2014 2293 7th graders	Internet addiction exacerbated depression, hostility and social anxiety
2016 Korean study of 1573 high school students	Internet addiction showed increased depression and suicidal ideation

Specific Learning Disorders

These occur in children with average or above average intelligence, with no sensory motor deficits and essentially receive normal schooling. The problems are in reading, writing, comprehensive and maths. Remedial packages can be tailored to suit the child's deficits profile. Children from disadvantaged background attending schools with poor infrastructure and poorly motivated and untrained teachers or absent teachers may show up as 'academically backward'. ASER 2010-2016 across the nation report that majority of the 6th standard children have language and maths skills of the second standard child. This learning deficit is caused by a poor education system and not SLD. The typical child with SLD would have always had it from the time of joining school. However, a recent onset of scholastic decline may occur due to psychological reasons.

Summary

- All the above disorders bear different diagnosis yet may overlap in a single child.
- There could be difficulties in oneself, school or home environment or both together may cause learning difficulties.
- Finding out multiple cases and working with specific strategies targeting the causes is essential. Recommended model is to use supportive techniques tailored to the needs of the individual child.

Nature of the BEAST
(Genie Out of the Bottle: IoT and AI)

INNOCUOUS PHOTOGRAPHS of pre-pubertal children romping around the swimming pools in their backyards may go on public domain through YouTube. This playground leaves a gate open for paedophiles. Despite many complaints from parents received by the company, it continues to send from its archives such videos through its automated viewing recommendation system. An innocent video becomes a part of our ever-increasing sexualised pornographic viewing. A viewer (in this case, paedophiles and kidnappers) can track the child and directly communicate with the child and lure him/her to sexual misadventures.

The controversy about parental applications reveals the ambivalence of Tech groups towards safety of children. They play the devil's advocate, saying that the child's privacy is breached by parents. Ultimately, who is responsible when disaster strikes a youngster? Take the instance of Ahmed, a 16-year-old, collapsing with a cardiac arrest after continuously playing of PUBG over several hours. The parent is held responsible. Never the game creators! They have ways and means to wriggle out of responsibility through legal means!

Nature of the beast is that it is a wolf in lamb's cuddly clothing!

The young get infatuated with the cuddly lamb and loath to part with it. The wolf inside actually harbours twin devils. Outreach by IoT and AI and advertising products such as junk food, aim to eliminate home-cooked and healthy food and increases the craving for branded clothing items, mobiles, cars, small toys and elaborate gaming techs.

This need eventually ends up in – unknown to the owner and the child – total surveillance of the victims, their desires and inclinations. For example, Google now feeds you stories from sites that you like, ...it follows the archeology or science websites you follow, and your newsfeed soon comprises such articles. Similarly, for product sellers, who eventually target parents of children and convince them to spend money on games, technology like smart phones, too add to the incredible wealth of the technology giants.

Are the technocrats aware of their power? Of course, they are. It is from the converted that the critic arises. They are called techno-skeptics. Ranks of critics, and their techno identity has expanded across political divides and it is due to these critics that the world is experiencing a sense that Facebook and Twitter, Google etc exert too much influence on the national discourse (Harman 2018). There is a widespread concern that we have developed unhealthy relationship with our phones and the applications on them.

Justin Rosenstein, the inventor of Facebook, called Facebook the 'Bright drug of pseudo pleasure' in 2017. In 2018, Jana Partners, a shareholder in Apple, wrote a letter to the company warning that its products may be having unintended negative consequences. These skeptics come from within the system.

Today there are warnings about addictive design tricks and project-driven systems influencing our minds. 'Red Dots' on the screen are suggestive of addictive application design. But is that sufficient warning?

Biddabi, in *New York Times*, highlights the Silicon Valley disruption of an Australian School in Williams Town, where there is no homework, no classrooms, no uniforms or traditional grades. The American Luminary model highlights that 'traditional schooling' is set in the era of post-industrial revolution, a 100 years ago. The Silicon Valley's efforts are the same as churning out new applications. There is a need for evidence-based research on long-term outcome of numerous applications. Educational programmes founded by Elon Musk (Tesla), Reed Hastings (Netflix), Mark Benioff of Salesforce, Alt School by Max Ventilla are the rave. These schools have used marketing buzz words like 'social' and 'emotional learning', mindset, grit, STEM, mindfulness, authentic learning, global consciousness.

The Truth about Technology

There is a national campaign in the USA called 'Truth about Tech', designed to expose the ways platforms like YouTube, Snap Chat, Facebook are harmful to children and to protect young minds from digital manipulation and exploitation. Organised by a nonprofit platform like Commonsense and Centre for Human Technology, this movement is often compared to the anti-tobacco awareness campaigns in the 1990s.

The truth campaign deals with deliberate use of designs aimed at promoting addiction. Tobacco campaigns were easier as the dangers were physically visible, while the effects of excessive media use are without any concrete physical evidence. Studies have shown that the amount of dopamine release in the brain while gaming is similar to that of drug addiction.

The Koepp study of 1998 showed that 2D video games raised dopamine levels in blood by 100 per cent and these were not even 3D virtual reality games. It has been even suggested that gaming could release endorphin too.

The question here is whether we should use something stronger than morphine to influence the brains and minds of seven years old or 14 years old? Would screens be as addictive as morphine?

Perhaps, it would be better to adopt the 'greater automobile safety' campaign model for the Truth about Technology movement rather than the anti-tobacco model. Both can provide solid evidence to win legal battles. Solutions are simple. 'Quit smoking or don't start smoking or do not speed, do not drink and drive' and so on are easy slogans. These simple efforts to counter technology's pervasive attack on humanity, especially children, are easily rebuffed by technocrats, leading to confusion among the parents. Let us have some examples to understand how helpless adults and the young users are in the face of massive technology invasions.

For example, 10 years ago, Pokémon Go became a rage while teenagers went outdoors to capture monsters. When they became addicted, the company defended it based on research, saying that it takes children outdoors. Following the yes-no debate on this particular game, children in the USA were instructed, 'Do not use Pokémon Go when high (on drugs)!' This cannot be a universal instruction as the game is played in diverse countries by diverse populations, and not all populations use drugs.

In India, a couple of years ago, 'Blue Whale' was a game that became popular, leading to suicides in many teenagers. The Government of India then banned it.

PUBG is another game very popular in India, causing concerns with long hours of gaming and behavioural problems seen among young adults, despite several State courts directing that the game be banned. However, the Supreme Court of India has revoked the State high courts' orders, on technical grounds.

With all the safety concerns in the real world, when one is attentive to it, one is forced to ask, is gaming a monster catching teenagers, unaware of safety hazards. The Young in India need better protections as tech gadgets are mass proliferating and net charges are low. The US campaign, 'Truth about Tech' needs to be replicated in India. In India, where poverty is still a reality, it is the issue of 'priority' that needs to be a matter of widespread debate, followed by awareness campaigns. Even in April 2020, one did get to read media reports on heart attack deaths due to constant and nonstop plying of PUBG.

And one need not be shocked by the news of a youth beheading his father for taking away his mobile and stopping his PUBG game. It is similar to alcoholics murdering family members if denied money to buy their supply. In serious cases of gaming addiction, before suddenly taking away the digital devices, the player must be psychologically prepared. This is true of especially the youth as they are strong enough to physically endanger others.

Then there are games and games. We have just named a few. There are scores of games where every action hero – like Batman, Superman is active, every Marvel comic hero and villain in an app attacks or saves the gamer. Spider Hero, Transformer are all popular games. There are simple games like Pick Up, or Temple Run 1 and 2 for 4 years old.

Even the Harry Potter book series, which many may consider 'innocuous' and 'harmless', has a series of games where the book characters are players and playing with the gamer. These are age-specific games, suited for toddlers to adults, their complexities in accordance. Time devoted, is also according to individual player's choice, but if you do not play specific actions within specific times, you can loose points – in that way, it is, and can be binding too. The Forts are public places, like restaurants, parks, metro stations and groups can play together. For eg, Shivaji Park, Mumbai is a favourite, I, the gamer can meet others playing too, the same game. All are Harry Potter fans and there is a considerable 'socialising' component, especially for single individuals. The negative impact is yet to be studied.

The companies grow so fast that it is impossible for the legal agencies to contain them. How do the game companies convince families? By assuring the mothers that giving more gadgets and screen time increases emotional bonding with the child. An adolescent would certainly like a mother who gives him a smart phone than one who does not, because they do not know better. A responsible mother does not fall for such propaganda and she understands the nature of the beast. She has to explain to the youngster the unnecessary and dangerous outcome of unlimited screen use.

Even the food industry is clever in the ways of advertising and hooking children with alternative jingles and gifts. For the unwary mother, there is an application showing how the child and mother cook together with KRAFT cheese. The trap is that you have to buy KRAFT cheese to interact with your own child!

Case 17

In a group of preschoolers, in a programme called philosophy for children, arranged at the Hawaii University, I witnessed the following sequence of interactions and communication. To the question on what they did that morning, one child said, 'Talked of the game of elaborate cooking on a cooking range, with complicated instruction for making imaginary tea'.

In the beginning children enjoyed the new toy and the game. Then gradually they discussed how they enjoyed or did not such a complex game. Finally, one child said, 'Making real tea is so easy. If we are all careful, we can make real tea and drink'. Perhaps we need to have 'philosophy for children' groups and discuss the pros and cons of mobile use, beginning with the preschoolers – as a realistic preventive effort.

I would like to provide two contrasts between two

preschoolers, one I saw a decade earlier in a remote rural area in South India and the other is Naina, a preschooler from Mumbai.

Case 18

I was studying and video-graphing child rearing practices in rural India. Lakshmi was three-and-a-half years old and was older of the two siblings. Her brother was one-and-a-half years old. She performed poorly on psychological assessment when she was shown pictures and asked to describe them, cut with scissors, recognise shapes etc. When I started observing her daily routine, I discovered that she would sweep her little hut with a broom, wash small dishes with wood ash (as in the local custom, all cooking was done on small wood fire clay stoves), rinse it neatly and invert them and keep them for drying. Then she helped her mother to bathe her baby brother. She was especially careful, keeping her palm above his eyes so that the soapy water from his head would not get into his eyes. She was playing the little mother. No, I do not think it is child labour. She joyfully shared her mother's daily chores.

In contrast, five-year-old Naina, an upper-class preschooler from one of the best preschool in Mumbai, told me that she loved YouTube and could make lot of things and was continuously viewing them on her iPad. She asked me for an envelope. I asked her to make one as it is so easy. I gave her an A4 size paper, gum and scissors. She could not do it, despite suggestions on how to fold the paper and cut it. In fact, she could not cut the paper. YouTube makes one think one has learnt to do some thing. But unless one actually does it, one cannot learn. In fact, electronic aid leads a child to be over-confident, without actually being able to do much.

How do ordinary parents fight the legal clout, wealth and lobbying of the Techno-Industries? Appeal to the humane aspects of these profiteers?

Fei-Fei Li's AI for All

In June 2017, Fei-Fei Li, a Stanford University scientist, presented herself before the US House Committee on Science, Space, and Technology. She was the only woman before that committee and the topic they were discussing and hearing was the good and the bad about 'Artificial Intelligence – With Great Power Comes Great Responsibility'. That June, Li was serving as the chief AI scientist at Google Cloud and was on leave from her position as director of the Stanford Artificial Intelligence Lab. But she was appearing in front of the committee because she was also the cofounder of a nonprofit focused on recruiting women and people of colour to become builders of artificial intelligence.

Li began working in Princeton on AI and building a database from eventually 15 million images. In 2012, Li joined Stanford, and lead the team that finally gave birth to Artificial Intelligence that could be used as a tool.

Deep learning systems are, as Li says, 'bias in, bias out'. Li recognised that while the algorithms that drive artificial intelligence may appear to be neutral, the data and applications that shape the outcomes of those algorithms are not. What mattered were the people building it and why they were building it.

It was critical, Li came to believe, to focus the development of AI on helping the human experience.

One of her projects at Stanford was a partnership with the medical school to bring AI to the ICU in an effort to cut down on problems like hospital-acquired infections. It involved developing a camera system that could monitor a hand-washing station and alert hospital workers if they forgot to scrub properly. This type of interdisciplinary collaboration was unusual.

That work gave Li hope for how AI could evolve. She felt, it could be built to complement people's skills rather than simply replace them. If engineers would engage with people in other disciplines (even people in the real world!), they could make tools that expand human capacity, like automating time-consuming tasks to allow ICU nurses to spend more time with patients, rather than building AI, say, to automate someone's shopping experience and eliminate a cashier's job.

By 2014 Li and Olga Russakovsky had launched the nonprofit 'AI4All' to bring underrepresented youth – including girls, people of colour, and people from economically disadvantaged backgrounds – to the campuses of Stanford and UC Berkeley to create what they called humane AI. Basically, the particular AI product parameters had to be in accordance with the following protocol:

How to Make AI human?[5]

1. Human centered AI (highlight the richness of human perception as a contrast).
2. AI's human connectedness is aimed at enhancing us and not replacing us – use in surgery, repetitive and monotonous jobs in countries where there is no one to do them **but not in countries where every job, no matter how dreary, keeps hunger away.** In India, the changing scenario of automation has already hit the labour market adversely. Only creative, intellectual and emotional roles cannot be fulfilled by AI. AI is limited by the limited brains of the team that put it together.
3. Assurances need to be there that the development of AI is grounded in the concerns on its effects on humans, especially children and the elderly.
4. AI cannot replace the collective wisdom, empathy and morality of the world.

Pitfalls noted are:

i. Adverse effects on labour in countries where there is high unemployment.
ii. Ill effects on unrepresented communities such as disabled, elderly and marginalised.

5 https://www.wired.com/story/fei-fei-li-artificial-intelligence-humanity/

iii. AI's voracious appetite for data and privacy rights, mainly due to wealth production through advertising and marketing.
iv. Geo-political implications of global intelligence.

As Li's personal story shows, AI has too many pitfalls. In 2016, Li joined Google as chief scientist for AI of Google Cloud, the company's enterprise computing business. Li wanted to understand how industry worked and to see if access to customers anxious to deploy new tools would shift the scope of her own cross-disciplinary research. Companies like Facebook, Google, and Microsoft were throwing money into AI in search of ways to harness the technology for their businesses. And companies often have more and better data than universities. For an AI researcher, data is fuel.

Initially the experience was enlivening. She met with companies that had real-world uses for her science. She led the rollout of public-facing AI tools that let anyone create machine learning algorithms, without writing a single line of code. She opened a new lab in China and helped to shape AI tools to improve health care. But soon, she found her work involved in controversy.

In 2018, Li was caught in Google's very public criticism over its Project Maven contract with the US Defense Department. The programme uses AI to interpret video images that could be used to target drone strikes; according to Google, it was 'low-res object identification using AI' and 'saving lives was the overarching intent'. Many employees, however, objected to the use of their work in military drones. About 4,000 of them signed a petition demanding 'a clear policy stating that neither Google nor its contractors will ever build warfare technology'. Several workers resigned in protest. Li's department administered Maven, and her emails were leaked to NYT. So far, she had been considered an 'ethical' scientist, working only for public good. Technology, however well-meaning, is a runaway science.

It can be misused and is. Li's example is a classic case.

One of the interesting reports is from Harvard University on the creation of AI Norman. The study created a robot and examined its psychiatric status. Norman is named after Norman Bates of Hitchcock's psycho-classic cult movie. AI Norman was instructed on situations from the game Reddit, dealing with violence and other disturbing scenes. AI Norman was tested with the Rorschach Test. Its responses were pathological, suggestive of suicidal and violent thoughts. AI can be made violent and destructive to human, animal, plants and environment in general. *The ultimate discretion rests with the person behind the particular AI.*

Are war games safe? What about collateral damage?

Are Boeing 747 safe? How can simple error destroy people?

Are drones safe? What about collateral damage and unintended human, political and military response? A destructive state of mind that controls AI is even more dangerous than a nuclear melt down.

Stanford University has created AI Almond to compete with Siri and Alexa, to protect the owner from snooping by the robots. Every damaging tech has to have an antidote ready! The ever-expanding colonisation by the IOT needs built-in restraints on misuse.

What should you do?

Children by nature are trusting of adults

- Tend to believe everyone
- Unsuspecting of hazards
- Vulnerable
- Take risks.

1. Secure the technology environment

- Use proper tools and licensed software
- Updates and patches
- Strong passwords
- Encourage children to share passwords with you

- Have child-friendly email ID
- Review Privacy settings
- Periodically review friend lists and posts.

2. Establish rules for posting, sharing and forwarding

- What can be posted and shared
- Challenges with deletion or removing posts
- Social profiting and related challenges
- Beware of GPS data and what data can provide about the child
- Meta data
- Sexting (child pornography)
- Bullying (IT Act provision)
- Use reasonable IT security practices (IT Act).

3. Understanding reporting options

- Do you have required information as evidence
- IMEI/MAC Number
- Service provider
- Contact details of cyber cell webs.

My description is drawn from an account by Sebastian Edassery, former cybercrime expert, at the Central Bureau of Investigations of India, CBI, a co-panelist, in my talk on Challenges of Digital Parenting. I gratefully acknowledge his inputs.

Online Solicitations: Protecting Children in a Digital Era

Some of the important issues to be noted:

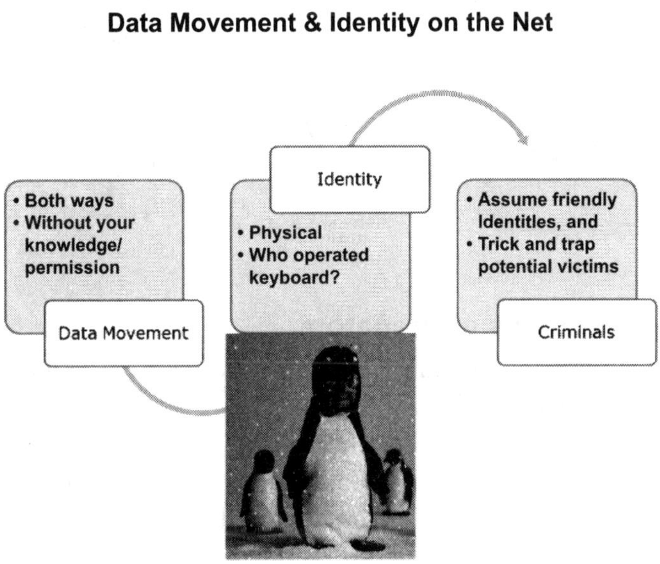

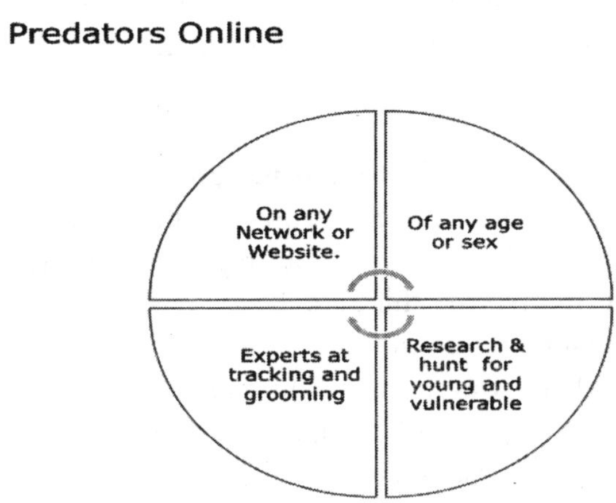

How do they identify & groom?

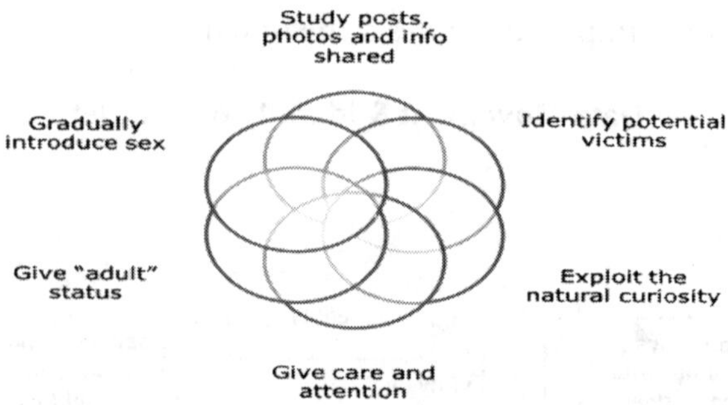

Warning Signs of Predators

- Exposing a child to things inappropriate to a child's age.
- Enticing with costly gifts.
- Threatening and blackmailing.
- Stressing on secrecy (threaten the children or families).
- Making children do uncomfortable things.
- Encouraging them to talk.

Nothing comes free in the world.

'Are the free cookies that are offered to you really free?' – should be the warning question to customers of all electronic products.

How does one deal with these situations?

- It takes a lot of courage to report to the government's Cyber Crime Department – but report it anyway.
- Do not frighten the children.
- Answer all their questions.
- Answer that it was not her or his fault.
- Give children patient hearing.
- Provide legal assistance.

Parental Controls & Netlingo

- 90% parents try to monitor children online, but 64% teens outwit them.
- 81% of children between 8 and 16 active on the Net and social media.
- 77% created Facebook/ social networking accounts before the age of 13.
- Issues of overreporting age

- ICT is a great tool. Criminal enterprise adapted it to their advantage like any other good tool/ technology.
- Teach children to use it safely
- Better get, buy-ins rather than enforcing control.

In summary:

- Create awareness
- Discuss best practices and challenges
- Establish expectations
- Self-consequence.

Technology cannot catch everything hence communicate. The earlier the better.

Have trusting and confiding relationship with your children so that when in danger, they will turn to you. Clive Thomson (2013) argues that keypad can be a tool to assist the disabled, digital tools such as smart phones and hard drives extend a mind and cognition, just as books did in the earlier era.

The Human Brain

Myelin and the role of myelination (white matter of the brain – gray matter – Bartzokis 2001) become very important as a 100 billion myelinated neurons form the brain.

Brain consists of gray matter, while myelination (the formation of myelin, a fatty substance sheath around the baby nerves that allows the baby nerve to transmit sensation, thought, feeling) that starts after the birth, establishes pathways to experience and learning in young children's development, in all the domains, physical, intellectual, language, cognitive, emotional, moral and sexual development. This is facilitated by the active use of all sensory modalities, namely visual, hearing (auditory), olfactory (smell), tactile (touch), gustatory (taste) as well as body movements (kinesthesis).

Thus, myelin enables the neurons speed up connectivity. These circuits – when used frequently – strengthen the pathways of an experience even in a young child. There is a difference in the brain of a child who is stimulated by enriching experience and a child who is exposed to impoverished environment with no stimulation. In the internet language, myelination increases the bandwidth. Language too is learnt very early in life. However, there is no doubt that both, **over stimulation** and **under stimulation,** are detrimental to optimal and normal brain development.

Devil's Advocate on Screen Use

An analysis of the data base from 1997-2017 was carried out by Nisha John et al (2019). The choice of video games was determined by age, gender, parental mediation, player characteristics as well as the game characteristics. The study showed that excessive gaming had negative impact on individual and interpersonal relationships. On the other hand, the benefits of gaming too were highlighted in this study.

The questions that arise here are what positive effects do gaming have and what promotive effects do habitual gaming have on the young? Excessive gaming has an addictive component of gamification and that needs to be kept in mind while promoting it. Perhaps conflict of interest – who provides the data with vested interests and who analyses it – supported by funding with conflict of interest need to be taken into account in such studies.

To demonstrate what we are up against when we try to deal with technology and when we try to reclaim childhood, I am citing here four websites with my comments highlighted in bold letters.

1. **A *Huff Post* website on 5 myths about technology** by Stephnie Dua and Keith Menacham, creators of Home Learn to Read programme. It says:

   i. All screen time is created equal (**of course, depends on the content**).
   ii. All screen time is bad for the brain, **exception** is when you use Home Learn to Read books.
   iii. Hard back books are better than e-books, but Home Learn to Read **is an exception!**
   iv. Children understand their parents' screen time. **No, they don't.** They are role models for their children's screen use.
   v. **The screen time takes away the child's interest in reality.** No, it acts as a supplement to natural curiosity.

Obviously Home Learn to Read app is one of the key solutions.

2. *The Guardian*'s Review says:

The consensus is that screen time, in and of itself, is not harmful – and reasonable restrictions vary greatly, depending on a child's behaviour and personality. There is little point in obsessing over how many minutes a day your kids are spending with screens. Instead, parents should be doing what they can to ensure that what they are watching, playing and reading is high-quality, age-appropriate and safe – and joining in wherever possible. **(*The Guardian* is my most favourite daily newspaper. The page quoted above, has requests for contributions to sustain Guardian's financial health.)**

3. Swaddle

It discusses the actual effects of screen time on kids' development. It is authored by the Swaddle team (2017).

It starts with a bright and rather strange picture of a baby lying down cross legged and watching a TV cartoon on the wall.

The short-term effects of screen time at 6 months is delayed cognitive development and at 2 years it is delayed cognitive and language development and language delays later on. Physical development is compromised with myopia or nearsightedness, which is reported in Australia, China and Thailand. Risk of obesity in children too is reported.

The emotional and social development are compromised as they are unable to transfer learning from the screen to real life. Screen time cuts down mother-child interaction and play. Behaviour problems seen are aggression, disobedience, cheating stealing and so on. Long term effects of screen time is associated with obesity, and sleep disturbance.

'In summary, multiple developmental and health concerns exist for children using all forms of digital media to excess', the team says.

But what is the hidden agenda behind this sage advice? It is followed by a You Tube advice by an Indian panel of experts. You are expected to buy the app. But what is not mentioned is, the huge Swaddle empire of numerous, expensive, desirable, non-essential baby objects that are catalogued and a mother will be tempted to buy! You, the reader is now on their mailing list.

4. Benedict Carey, a science writer, in the December 2018 ***New York Times*** issue highlights the largest ever study by the US National Institutes of Mental Health (NIMH) termed, Adolescent Brain Cognitive Development Study (ABCD). This study on brain functions proposes to assess every year the functional Magnetic Resonance Imaging FMRI of 11,800 children, started in 2013 in 21 centres. It initially aimed at studying the impact of alcohol and drug abuse, later went on to include screen time, genetics and array of environmental factors.

i. In 2018 early trends on 4,500 pre-teens trend were discussed in a CBS 60 minutes programme. Because of the diversity of findings the study, so far, cannot confirm that screen time is bad; measured effect may even be good, until definitive answers emerge over a period of several years when this remarkable study is completed.

The result so far has somewhat assuaged the fears of parents.

a. 43 studies reported that there is a widening of circle of social contacts which is a good thing, though these may also include abuse content.
b. 200 studies on screen time conclude violent video viewing is connected to aggressive behaviour. The finding does not prove it is a causal relationship. The explanation being that the children with propensity for aggressiveness tend to view more violent content.

My own observation is that in social sciences, correlation does not mean causality. Do we negate results of all the other studies indicating the need for setting limits to screen time? These are trends to be confirmed or otherwise.

ii. Even if there is a single measurable effect such as three hours of screen time **leads to ADHD, this does not necessarily lead to measurable effect on the brain.**

Lack of definite evidence in the early stages (as in the case of smoking and cancer) may allow strong lobbies demanding unequivocal and strong evidence. But we owe children some intuitive caution while waiting for hundred per cent proof.

iii. Individual brain variations in the brain structure is so much that huge number of subjects are recommended and better understanding of the adolescent brain.

The presence of multiple aetiological factors may cloud the results. Correlations do not imply causation. Do we wait for the final and definitive results? Like in climate change issue, the events may overtake us before we agree whether the concept is a *fictional entity* as many climate skeptics believe. In case of our children, I would like to err on the side of caution.

5. There is an interesting hypothesis called Goldilocks Hypothesis. Proposed by research studies in Oxford University, UK this alludes to the Goldilocks story where the little girl visits the three bears and tasting their porridge finds, one bowl too hot, another too cold and the third one just right! In their study of wellbeing of English adolescents and their screen use, Przybylski and Weinstein in 2017 noted (n:120,115) that moderate use of digital technology is not intrinsically harmful and may be advantageous in a connected world. The mental wellbeing went down with little use, rose with certain amount and then started to drop.

They also make a valid point to further study the impact of these recreational activities, involving TV or videos, playing video games, general computer uses and smart phone, needed to be examined among other daily pursuits such as sleep and eating. The original study recommends limiting adolescents' technology use and advocate rigorous investigations into the realties between digital world and children's and adolescents' health and wellbeing. In another study by the same team in 2019, of 17,000 people in the UK, the effect size (a statistical measure) on wellbeing was claimed to be imponderably high. This demolished the claim that digital world has any impact on adolescent wellbeing and health.

Are the authors justified in coming to a conclusion based on a very large number of subjects, adopting quantitative statistical analysis? What effects do other variables – when the other daily pursuits like diet, sleep, exercise etc – have when the same statistics is applied? In qualitative analysis, even a single case can provide valid insights to enable us to help the child.

In summary, we need to be aware of the nature of the impact of IOT/AI. They are not altruistic, they create wealth for themselves, while cause unseen damage to our children, physically and psychologically. In the long run, protection of children from the lit up screens and monitors is our duty.

Advertising: The Trojan Horse

WE GO back to the old Greek story, how a large wooden horse (which hid a number of enemy soldiers) was given as a gift to the defenders in the city of Troy, thus defeating the Trojans by deception. Advertisements have existed across the world from early times onwards in human history. In earlier times, town criers were hired to inform people of a forthcoming event and was, in its rudimentary form, information dissemination.

As an industry, it became popular with the advent of print, radio and television platforms. The British Parliament passed legislation in 1974 to protect children from efforts by merchants to sell their products. Commercial exploitation of children happened with advent of cable television, with child-oriented channels exploiting the children through catchy jingles and attention-seeking visual clips. Now there are numerous child-oriented websites. The fact is that even adults succumb to this exploitation, they are in no position to guard themselves from it. In fact, children use 'pester power' to get the parents to buy whatever they want. Terms like 'shopaholics' and 'retail therapy' are used to describe adult advertisement-prompted addictions.

In the earlier days, the family shared the viewing of TV or listening to radio and the programmes were limited and few. This, in fact, facilitated family quality time. But with exclusive marketing, TV, PC, iPads and mobiles have become easily available. The tragedy of the powerful marketing approach has changed peoples' lifestyles, especially in poor countries. So much so that everyone now has TV but often at the cost of not having a toilet/bathroom and even a kitchen. The TV and techno gadgets have become a status symbols even among the poor. Among the rich, it has led to spouses viewing different programmes while each child is given his own space, surrounded by techno gadgets. This has led to drastic reduction in the time the family spends together. This proves the point that the digital addiction leads to isolation rather an attachment and cohesion. Many children have unsupervised access to digital devices.

With the advent of interactive digital toys (games), with their inbuilt specific addictive content and form, they now become available to children at a much younger age than ever before. Now these iPads, smart phones and Xboxes have becomes forms of digital drugs, advertising make it to your children through extensive use of private data, targeting the very population we need to protect.

Today, the techno-cautious parents belong to the domain of the Beast. Yet, they all protect their own children from these manipulations by their own industry

For example, Steve Jobs was a notoriously low-tech parent. The techno founders themselves went to low tech schools and send their children to low tech schools. Many parents do understand intuitively that the glowing screens have adverse effects on their children. Does their collective conscience not prick them, when other people's children are deliberately damaged? Perhaps they dehumanise other people's children and believe that everything is fair in war and profiteering! Is that why some turn into magnanimous corporate funders to various large charities to wash off their sins? Is it blood money they are dealing with?

Advertising channels directly reach children, as advertisers spend more than 12 billion dollars per year for the youth market and children view more than 400,000 commercials. This puts them at risk from several dangers.

Advertising affects children. How they affect the children depends on their age and stages of cognitive, language, emotional, social and moral development. Up to the age of three, they cannot understand that objects or screens on the TV are not real. They also cannot differentiate between actual programmes and advertisements.

Body Language

Competition has a language. The Desire to win. The Aggression to win. The Hard Work to win. The Elation on success. The Despondency on failure. All these expressions of human emotion form the body language of competition.

Advertisements also have a body language. It always says, if you use product x-y-z you are Better, you are Bigger, you are Stronger, you are Taller. There is always a Yardstick, a Measure. You – mostly the child and his/her parent – have to measure up on this social Yardstick. It is a competition in 'being' – being worthwhile. The parent has to prove he/she is a better parent if they give the child an ipad or smart phone. The child has to measure up to his/her peers by possessing a smart phone. It is not even a boiled sweet or toffee that proves a person's worth. It is a gadget, not a bicycle but a electronic device. It is not just a mobile phone, it is the kind of phone that is the determiner of social standing. This social standing even cuts across digital divide. It cuts across priorities.

A poor mother needs a smart phone as the children want a smart phone for video calls to grandparents, cousins. There is, theoretically, nothing wrong in that. Technology has helped remote access. But the same smart phone allows the children to play PUBG and see the Boost or Bournvita advertisement, beyond the reach of the poor mother. There are other dangers too from such ads.

Not long ago, Bournvita had a quiz competition. It was a school-based programme and, of course, the booster drink was promoted in all schools participating. They were, naturally, all schools for the middle-income group, where parents could afford to feed their kids, the booster drink. The company also supported school sports days and competitions, promoting the booster. However, as the number of television channels in the country and channels for children increased, it took quickly to television promotion of its various products. Popular heroes were roped in.

Other similar companies too followed. Boost, Horlicks and several others. Shaktiman showed off his six-pack abs. It often appears, as if only children who drink Bournvita or Boost or Horlicks are the children who grow. The same message is conveyed with the Dabur Chawanprash ad. Only those children are worth nurturing who 'grow' Strong, Tall, Smart. All others do not count. Poor children who have no access to these products, have no chance to thrive in life – this message comes forth loud and clear. However, this negative signal such ads give out is never discussed in the public domain. There are other issues too.

Cadbury, three-four years ago, had started a campaign on 'sharing', for teenagers…a boy enticing a girl with a chocolate. It was a lovely ad no doubt. The body language of the two protagonists of the ad leapt off the screen, it was unmistakable. However, it is very difficult to explain what happens on screen to a seven or ten-year-old viewer and consumer of the same chocolate.

Ads like the Flipkart are no doubt amusing. But it is very difficult to explain them to ten-year olds. The caricatures represent people...a father or mother or uncle or aunt figure. The voices are children's. But they are talking a mix of adult and children's lingo. Then there were ads with miniature caricature figures, representing children who speak in adult voices. The companies, Flipkart and Happy Creatives, both said, recall was high, it was funny. Flipkart, those days, was just a delivery company. The recall factor was for the brand – Flipkart. But who was it for? The child or the parent? The ad, in family viewer programmers, was utterly inexplicable to young viewers. What did they actually say? Was it necessary to involve children's caricatures or voices at all in the ads? Ten years on, in the face of competition from Amazon and Alibaba, does anyone remember Flipkart because of that series of advertisements?

A Surf washing powder ad says, '*Dag acche hai*'. Yes. True. The mother has to scrub more after a child turns up with such a splash. Perhaps a washing machine and continuous water supply is needed. Also, if '*Dag acche hai*' – why teach children to be spic and span, wear clean clothes? Stains are good – so why teach a child to be neat and clean? And how does a mother explain to her ten-year-old, he/she must not stain his clothes, make clothes dirty? One can never explain away detergent ads.

Just as one cannot explain diaper ads. Pampers, Poko Pants ads promote the discrimination – good mother-bad mother. Can a mother ever be judged on the basis of nappy use? Should a mother be judged by this? What about Indian mothers who have been lauded for thousands of years without diapers? The slogan on TV is '*poori raat diaper pehnaiye - chain ki neend paaiye*'. It conveys two messages for the parent – the baby can sleep peacefully or the mother can sleep as she does not have to wake to change the nappy. Diapers, as a result, may not be changed for 12 hours from 8pm to 8am. Ignore such basic things as hygiene, nappy rash, aeration of baby skin. Whose good sleep is important? And what about the poor mother, who cannot buy a diaper to use all night, not even for a few hours in the day? One is not even asking if such television ads are contributing to the social and economic divide?

Take for instance one of the most alluring ads with Big B trying to fit on a child's pretty shoes for an online store First Cry. When a five-year old sees the advertisement, she wants a pair of shoes just like that. Affordability? All little girls want to be Barbie dolls, irrespective of the economic divide. Why shout at poverty from the rooftop?

The promotion of educational apps like Byju's are even more surprising.

Byjus partnership with Disney for young kids promotes the idea that kids learn from an app and that Disney is attractive content for kids. Two entities have teamed up here. Both have global reach. And apps like this, promoting remote learning, are more or less destined to replace all teacher student interaction – something real students and real teachers cherish. In this condition of a lockdown of more than a million schools under a pathogen attack, the virtual teacher is soon going to permeate all teaching activity across ages. Yet a six-year-old continues to assert, the real classroom is more interesting, more fun. The body language of the teacher and the students in a real classroom cannot ever be transmitted through a computer screen. To add to the untruth, remote learning content providers now have yet another slogan, this time for real teachers, 'blackboard use is a waste of time'.

Even non-banking financial entities like SBI securities advertise 'smart decisions' featuring children. India knows, the young are consumers. It is not bothered about how the ad impacts children, it wants to grab parent attention – buy it, be it chocolate for the child or security bonds. Especially when there is no actual regulator, neither government, nor parental bodies, nor teacher groups. No 'truth about Technology' lobbies here.

Young Children and Advertising
Case 19

At 0 to 2 years, children cannot differentiate between advertising and actual events. I recall a little girl who constantly sang a jingle that went with sanitary pad advertisements. In movie theatre, she sang out the name of the brand with joy at seeing her favourite advertisement. In India, even babies are taken to the movies and allowed to watch TVs at home with adults. They absorb everything about the storyline and advertisements.

At 3 to 6 years, they can understand these two are different, but are not aware of what or whom the advertisements are aimed at. For example, there are very attractive and catchy advertisements of Alexa and mobile devices. These give multiple and different messages to the child and the parents. For example, a girl is enjoying Alexa singing, 'Old McDonald had a farm'. The father enters, after a long and tiring day at the office. He sinks into the sofa and says, 'Alexa, what's the news?' Alexa stops the nursery rhyme and starts the news. The little girl pouts and pulls a long face. The father looks at her and orders Alexa to go back to the nursery rhyme.

I would like you to be sensitive to the hidden message, behind the 'buy Alexa' theme. When father comes home, the child pays no attention to him. He, in turn, pays no attention to her, nor greets or hugs her. They are in competition; he wants news and she wants nursery rhymes. He yields, giving the message to us that we should yield to the child. Are we talking about a battle of wills here?

In a normal home, I would like the mother to be singing along with the child. I, as a young mother, knew nursery rhymes in my mother language, and not in English. My husband and I had different mother tongues and had no common Indian language. So, we spoke in English to each other. I learnt all the English nursery rhymes, with my daughter singing along and acting them out. I vividly recall both of us on our fours, having a go at 'Old McDonald'. It was a time when, if the father comes in, he too could join in. Mother would say, Daddy has come and the child would run to him and he would lift her and they would talk. As the parents settle, they would talk about the day and ideally, the little one would join in, telling them about her day at school. Please do not ask, why I was at home? As a professional psychologist, I have always worked, but made time for my children, putting career aspirations on the back burner till they went off to higher grades. In short, Alexa comes in the way of healthy interactions between parents and a child.

In most advertisements, there is only one child. There is no space for siblings or grandparents. Promotion of selfishness and self-centeredness seems to be the second message.

I have seen advertisements for mobiles, where the child plays one parent against the other, talking over the mobile. The message is that the viewer should buy a particular brand of mobile. The message is, the parents are in competition and use devious means to get what you want.

The soft targets are children in the advertising world, be it foods, snacks, supplements, chocolates and so on. Home-cooked food is fast vanishings from the scenario. The child is supposed to become stronger, tall, smarter with what is shown in the advertisements. Here too, attempt is made to show children who cannot get the advertised products as inferior in a very active and persuasive manner, be it the father's new car, high-end gadgets, toys, clothes and so on.

This age is particularly vulnerable.

Ways to Limit Viewing Advertisements

i. Cut down the TV screen time.
ii. Buy TV shows, DVD etc without advertisements.
iii. Watch the advertisements and programme, analyse its hidden message and tell your child and allow your child to watch programmes suitable for that age group, keeping in mind the child's developmental domains. Allow only suitable programmes you have personally screened, but not recommended by those who are paid

heavy amounts to advertise and reviews of gadgets in professional manner, covertly promoting the item.

Primary School Children and Advertising (7 to 11 Years)

They can understand that advertisements are used to sell something. They can remember the advertisements more than their class lessons, as they listen to them repeatedly. They can even see how the advertisements exaggerate the qualities. Like images of giant of a man after taking supplements. They do not question these directly.

A young couple had a son in this age group who was spending long hours with TV viewing, with both parents at work. The concerned parent asked his son to list 10 good things about TV. The parents rejoiced when the boy brought the list. The list contained 10 bad things about TV and nothing good. His TV viewing dramatically reduced following this exercise.

Parents can also actually take each of the advertisements and discuss them, but it is better to focus on the advertisements which are watched most frequently. For example, tell the child what the product is, who and what is it for. For example, a packet of Lays chips works out one rupee for a chip, while standard local freshly made chips are lot cheaper. So, pointing out that junk foods contribute largely to profit through advertisements is important.

This is an active campaign about home-cooked food. Parents in India are very concerned about their child's eating and believe that poor eating in the child is due to bad mothering. In a clinical setting, hardly ever food fads or poor eating is presented as a complaint. Most often when asked, the mother says that he eats very poorly. When asked what he normally eats, it comes out that he eats chocolates, chips and often junk food. Junk food fetish is entirely due to advertisements.

Adolescence and Advertising (12 to 16 years)

They understand the purpose of advertisements. They ask themselves how real is the lifestyle being advertised. Do people you see live like that, dress or eat like that? Are the food and drinks advertised healthy? Do body-shaming, fairness creams or soaps really work? These advertisements, for example promote the ideas about what is beautiful or what is to be achieved. Body shaming consists of showing some one as fat or with darker skin tones as undesirable. The idea is to promote slender body and fair skin. This could mean promoting the sales of dietary supplements or fairness soaps/creams. Body shaming of young boys or girls too is often seen.*

However, obviously, the attempt is to sexualise the younger adolescents. Deodorants, shaving creams, flashy clothes are all ways of influencing them to look like grown ups. But, why? Why cause the loss of innocence so early in life?

The worse culprits are the 'Reality Shows' for young adolescents. No one dares to question them as they are very popular. They are sexualised so early that even a three-year-old indulges in seductive dances. She is applauded. Are there no rules as to what age-appropriate body movements, gestures and expressions of emotion are? Should everyone do item dances, mimicking voluptuous female body contortions? These pre-pubertal children are made to drape themselves around grown adults, as the two perform together. Have you examined ill effects of early sexualisation? There is no end to the sexual exploitation carried out in the name of talent scouting.

Some Common Advertising Strategies – Know that:

- Free toy when the child or parent buys a product is a bribe.
- Free game when child or parent buys a toy.
- Big or false claim, that this product is the best.
- Child or buyer's heroes like a sports person or a film star promotes a product, so it must be good. The product seller has paid huge amounts of money to the hero to use his/her image in order to make you buy the product, as your hero worship, your favourite

cartoon character can make you buy toys and tee shirts depicting buyer's hero/the child's hero.

- Special effects produced in photography can make a product fantastic; online buying always makes product look good. It is only when one actually sees, touches and judges it in a different background that one can get an idea of what it is actually in reality.
- Repetition enhances memory. What one sees and hears very frequently is something when one goes shopping, even if one does not need it. A comparable product could even be much cheaper.
- Catchy music too can make one buy the product.
- Some of the advertisements capitalise on sense of humour. The classic examples are that of fevicol adhesive in India. One cannot think of buying another brand.

However, all the products, especially the techno devices, are exceedingly persuasive and are even designed to be addictive. Gaming is one such example. All interactive games are addictive, children are persuaded to pester their parents and buy them. Remember the BEAST breathes through advertising.

I will quote one study which reflects the complexity of the issues being discussed, be it the content of the Internet communication or of the advertisements.

The conflict of interests of the funders of any research is rarely discussed. Often, the conflict of interest of these research efforts show that conclusions do have a hidden agenda of promoting the positive impacts while making the results opaque in terms of economical, psychological and social aspects that are compromised in the various studies. Thus, any research results need to be evaluated by us with caution. Just remember the Trojan Horse when you get taken in by advertisements and commercials.

---

* The government in India has banned the promotion of the phrase 'Fair and Lovely' in the brand beauty product.

Collusion between Technology Industry and Education

NO DOUBT there are advantages in getting our own youngsters exposed and trained in the latest technological innovations. This is especially so in terms of future occupations in the technology realm. It is also important to assure that there are no digital divides in our future generation. But we need to know what the optimal level and overstimulation are.

Let me first bring you down to the reality of the school systems in India. Majority of our disadvantaged children go to government-run schools. These schools are aimed at promoting mass education. Unfortunately, these are beset by the problems of poor infrastructure (mainly, the absence of electricity renders technology-driven gadgets useless).

Poorly trained teachers insisting on rote learning and copying is yet another problem. The children are typically characterised by multiple diversities, divided by language, religion, socio-economic status, mental health issues, disabilities and so on. *No centralised teaching formula or A1 model can accommodate multiple diversities at the grassroots level.* Both private and public schools contribute to the wealth-production of the techno industry through buying expensive gadgets which often need upgrading. People with the knowhow cannot be accessed at the grassroots level.

Private school managements make children buy whatever is the latest in the gadgetry. The government schools, in an attempt to imitate the private schools, provide free computers to rural and urban government schools. The first 'Hole in the Wall'[6] was a successful experiment in producing computer literacy for slum children.

However, after decades of fun fare and publicity, it remains at present merely a Hole in the Wall according to Kentaro, the author of *Geek Heresy*. The computers supplied to the rural schools become computer graveyards due to lack of instructors, upgrades for the equipment or maintenance, most importantly due to lack of supply of electricity during the day despite rural electrification. Nevertheless, computers get supplied as it benefits the middlemen who procure them.

It is believed that once a gadget is supplied, it will be in perpetual use. Don't we all know the tedium of maintenance even in urban pockets supposedly filled with techno experts?

---

6 *The acquisition of basic computing skills by any set of children can be achieved through incidental learning provided the learners are given access to a suitable computing facility, with entertaining and motivating content and some minimal (human) guidance.*
A technology professor, Sugata Mitra, Chief Scientist at NIIT, is credited with the discovery of Hole-in-the-Wall. As early as 1982, he had been toying with the idea of unsupervised learning and computers. Finally, in 1999, he decided to test his ideas in the field. On 26th January, Mitra's team carved a 'hole in the wall' that separated the NIIT premises from the adjoining slum in Kalkaji, New Delhi. Through this hole, a freely accessible computer was put up for use. This computer proved to be an instant hit among the slum dwellers, especially the children. With no prior experience, the children learnt to use the computer on their own. The model has been replicated in several places.

All the technologies need constant and expensive upgrades, requiring expert advice. Can these happen in the remote villages of India? Then there is a major issue of safe disposals or recycling of the discarded gadgets – e-waste mountains are almost similar to nuclear waste and disposal is a huge problem.

Now we come to the schools, public or non-aided or even aided schools. There are edusat programmes beamed into classrooms. Most of these are poorly executed and packaged. There are videos and other modes to attract children in the classroom, iPad for story reading. Unfortunately, all children prefer the entertainment aspects of the iPad rather than the actual stories. It is used only about 15 per cent of the time for educational inputs. A blackboard with chalks is inexpensive and lasts for decades. It is a centuries-old tested tool.

Maths Teaching and Learning through Internet

As the primary school children in the government schools find maths to be the most difficult subject, I analysed the maths syllabus from class 1 to 5. I attempted to simplify it and make it part of the child-centred play way model.

To sum it up simply, the children from 1 to 5 class are expected to be able to do the following:

From ages 5 to 10 years, they are expected:

1. To learn the numbers, 1 to 9 in class 1, 10 to 20 in class 2, 21 to 30 in class 3, 1 to 100 in class 4 and 1 to 999 in class 5.
2. Read the clock.
3. Read the days, months and years.
4. Name the Body parts.
5. Name the Colours.
6. Name the Seasons.
7. Measurement cm/inch, metre/yard, kilometer/mile.
8. Weight litre/millilitere (volume) grams/kilograms (solid).
9. Lines and geometric shapes.

My team was able to get the children to grasp most of the concepts through action songs, nursery rhymes, stories, paper models, blocks, rings, coloured shapes and so on.

As a specific example of geometric shapes, given below is an example of online teaching of geometric shapes:

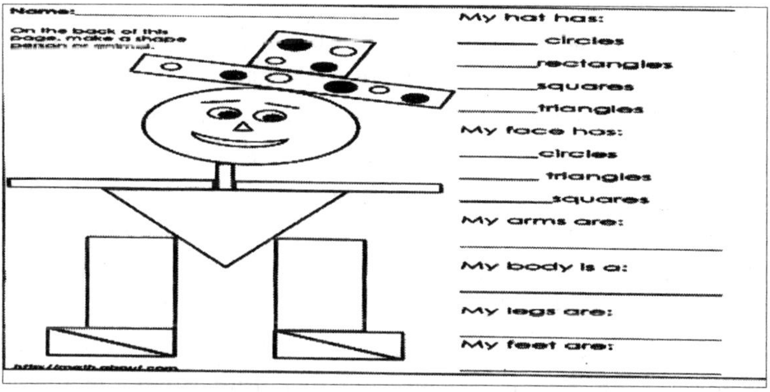

It is obvious that the shapes are introduced on a robot-like figure. It is supposed to represent a human being. A human figure obviously does not have geometric shapes of perfect circles, rectangles, triangles and so on. Is it possible for a first grader to understand this specimen figure?

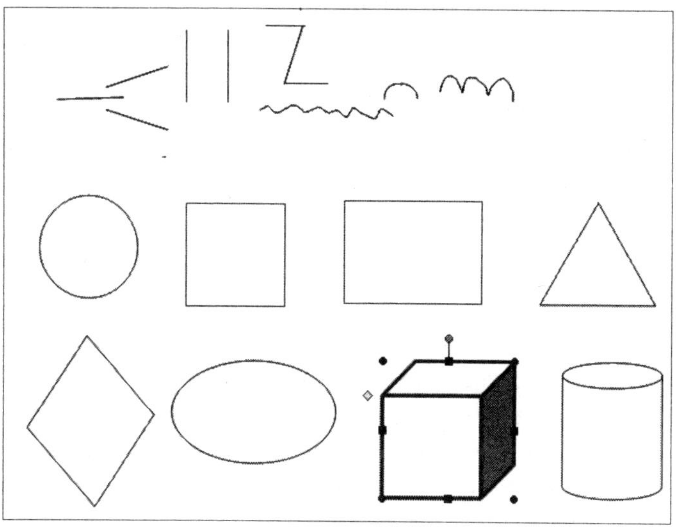

What we do in reality is either draw all the shapes on a black board, KG cardboard, or provide wooden blocks of different shapes. We show the circle and ask, 'What is this?' The children shout back 'Circle' or round in English or the appropriate word in their own languages. The group learns the term in English and in other languages.

Then we ask them to look around and report where they see this shape or even name the objects that they know, of this shape. They excitedly reply, 'Ball, moon...... laddoo...' and point to all the circular objects and shapes in their immediate environment. The most fascinating was their response to the oval shape. First there was silence. Then one child shouted, 'Soap'. They had identified with an oval cake of soap they were familiar with. The other children soon began to identify other oval objects with the shape; they happily joined the game of identifying similar objects. We then told them the shape was called oval. Interestingly, Indian sweetmeats provide a large number of shapes, including round, square, rectangle, diamond, oval, triangle and so on with 3D properties.

In another example, all the children of class 5 were asked to fold A4 size paper into shapes of whatever they wished. One girl made a paper boat. Many others too followed her. One boy was unable to and was sad. We asked the girl who made the boat to help him. She started not only to show how to fold but also added saying 'now this is a rectangle, next-a square and the next a triangle' and so on. It was all so simple! When you adopt a child-centred methods, you discover how innovative they all are!

Another example is the link between gadgets and advertisement, suggesting a strong collusion between industry and marketing. The children in higher classes are expected to do projects. These projects are made by googling the information, preparing power point presentations or actual models or printouts of the experiment in question. Advertisements by the HP printer, enticingly cheap, with colour prints are advertised and the parents are forced to buy them. Why not have the student draw, colour and actually craft the objects with material around such as cardboards, staples, gums, cello tapes etc. Why is preformed material considered superior to individually created creative efforts by your child?

How do we Remember What we Study?

The nature of how one remembers school subjects has undergone a revolution. In earlier times, one read the text books and the teachers helped us to understand it. Then it changed to teacher's giving notes, and especially emphasising what is likely to come in the forthcoming examinations, as pass percentage of a school decided its popularity. Then tuitions were added on, more as a bribe to the regular teachers for supporting their pupils. Then came the so called 'guides', which made a mockery of the textbooks. With the advent of photocopying, everything changed. One did not have to work at all. Making notes and remembering the subject became a lost art.

Now we have the final solution. Everything can be googled. Recently it was reported that a child asked Alexa to do her homework.

What happens to your brain if you don't learn or memorise?

Recently, glowing tributes were paid to charity-minded people in the technology sector, who installed an 'Echo'/Alexa system inside a shop mannequin and gave it to a rural school as a robot teacher. It caused a lot of excitement indeed! But can it ever be a substitute for a real teacher?

'Use your brain or lose it is the important message'. How many of you remember how to do sums without a calculator? Remember a frequently used phone number, your sibling's address or birthday? How to orient yourself, if you are lost in a place?

Uses of Technology in Education and Who Benefits? Let us examine what techno skeptics themselves think and do? A person like Jobs has said, what is wrong with education cannot be fixed with technology.

A comic strip by Roz Chast (2017 NYT) shows the stages of me and the TV! Infancy when TV makes no sense, childhood (griping about not having enough TV access), adolescence, the young adult, women and middle age, the lost years immersed in popular TV. The last one, a person in bed with Headgear with two words `Virtual Reality' (NYT on technology).

But the promotion by the industry is so powerful that how can the parents resist such schools? In Bangalore, the Silicon Valley of India, Narayana Techno Schools have their pupils ending up in our clinic.

Anya Kamenetz (NYT, Sunday, 4 March 2018) says your kids' phone is not like a cigarette.

Though there are arguments in favour of augmented technology, these are redundant in the Indian schools where the quality of education offered, especially in public schools as against private schools, is abysmally poor. The private schools are flush with funds. Tech use is a status symbol and costs are forced on to wealthy parents while the industry profits.

In the poor schools, the government spends scarce money it can hardly afford. In addition is the problem of corrupt practices in obtaining and maintaining tech gadgets. It is not only the schools that take pride in the tech gadgets, even parents share it. They claim that *it is needed* for schoolwork and for ensuring a bright future in the techno savvy world.

In an article on the 'Role of technology in Indian schools', astute observations on technology in the classrooms have been made by the renowned educationist, Prof Krishna Kumar (*The Hindu*, 12 January 2019). In remembering late Vijaya Mulay, whose contribution to the national policy on technology in education by the NCERT, he lauds her vision. She believed that technology must promote paucity of its use and promote creative endeavour.

Technology centralises decision-making and that in turn marginalises teachers. The teacher faces twin challenges – the teacher becomes dependent on technology and is, at the same time marginalised. Fight between ever-increasing new gadgets, applications-produced lessons and tests, along with surveillance of teachers is a battle of strong technology and weak teacher and mesmerised pupils. Technology is a double-edged sword. Even distance education programmes are neither rewarded nor helpful.

Mulay had warned against the tendency of using technology for **magnifying and replicating** entrenched systemic weaknesses. She believed in giving teachers status, and believed knowledge brought to life through technology to be irrelevant in an educational scenario. The present Covid19 pandemic has evidenced significant number of children and adults under lockdown conditions who have been overwhelmed by excessive online exposure.

The downside of technology is not allowing the child to be a child. Play, which promotes overall development, is a fact that is completely overlooked. Child-centred play is neglected and tech-centred one-way, top down lesson is what is provided to children through various electronic devices. Let children play in the real world instead of virtual world. Let us not make money out of depriving children from what they need and deserve – Real Play.

PART II

Interventions for 0 upto 4 Years

MOST OF the human brain's development is completed in this age group.

Brain development being at its peak in the newborn to preschooler, effect of screen time on their brain, and consequently, on their mind, leads to some important suggestions towards prevention and intervention at this stage.

Myelination occurs at a very rapid rate in infancy and childhood, becomes almost complete by the time the child is of seven years. In the internet language, myelination increases the band width of the brain.

If the child is **under-stimulated,** myelination does not occur adequately as in the case of children growing up in isolation, deprived environments.

In contrast, neuroscientists point to the evidence that **overstimulation** is equally damaging by being at too fast a pace to the growing brain.

Thus, below the age of seven years (for normal myelination is yet to be completed) the child should experience normal environment. This has to include physical and psychological bonding with the caretaker. The caretaker has to talk, making eye contact with the child, read, sing or tell stories to the child and most importantly, play with the child. The following section will give some anecdotal stories, case reports and outcome research of some intervention in the age group of 0 up to 4.

This is a stage where caretakers may or may not be familiar with use of technology. Is the caretaker a tech (digital) immigrant (new to technology) or as tech native as the child?

A poor illiterate mother is full of admiration for her tech native young child. However, whether it is tech savvy or tech immigrant, the child knows how to expertly manipulate the gadgets available with nimble fingers, clicking, tapping, swiping with ease. This leads to excessive screen time use, for example, while eating being involved with gadgets rather than parents or peer group.

A mother's indulgence and pride itself is an incentive to the child who does not know any better. On the other hand, tech native parents of the middle class ignore the anxiety of not providing quality time consisting of reading stories, playing or taking the child outdoors or to meet other children. Consequently, in either case, the child is over stimulated, leading to deficient myelination.

This is a serious concern to the growing brain. It brooks no negotiation regarding how helpful technology is for this. A mother singing nursery rhyme with the child is far superior to that of Alexa repeating it monotonously. While the mother and child can act out the nursery rhyme, be it *Old McDonald* or *Here, we go round the mulberry bush* or a more plebian *Nani Nani Suno Kahani, Ek thaa Raja, Ek thi Rani* or *Nila Nila Odi*

Vaa. It makes a big difference to the brain development at this crucial phase.

Some guidelines for weaning very young children from toxic technology in view of the dangers to the developing brain:

1. Minimise exposure to screens before seven years.
2. Delay the supply of digital toys as late as possible. Conventional building blocks, stuffed animals, conventional board games and toys should be the norm.
3. Replace fast screen activities with relaxed play with slow activities alone, with parents and other children.
4. Make activities child-centred and not screen-centred for your child.
5. Participate in conventional activities like family meals, outings, visits to families and friends, interaction with grandparents and so on.

Speech and Language Delays

In my own practice, I have witnessed speech delays in three children exposed to screen time early at the critical phase of language acquisition. These children had associated symptoms such as poor eye contact, temper tantrums and stubbornness. The parents were asked to stop the access to screen time.

In our experience, *complete stopping of screen time is possible* and though parents had reservations because of the child's anger outburst, we gave instructions to caretakers in numerous ways in the presence of the child, explaining why screen time should be stopped. This makes the parents empowered as they too realise, they could have attempted this approach earlier. Interestingly, grandparents, when present, always intuitively linked such delays with the parents' obsession with technology and their always seeking answers to all the difficult behaviours, on the internet. Most often, we found that the grandparents' experiential advices were always ignored, as parents and grandchildren were internet savvy.

Where are the Cockroaches?
Case 1

Anbu was a three-year-old child, when I first saw him. His mother was very anxious that he could not speak or make articulate speech. He made some sounds with such speed that no one was able to understand what he said. His movements also were very fast. He was unable to be in one place for a few minutes.

The mother had said that he did not make eye contact. But he was talking to me, looking straight at my face. So, I ruled out her fear of ASD (Autism Spectrum Disorder). He was under treatment at AIISH (All India Institute of Speech and Hearing), Mysuru for his speech remediation. The mother was afraid that he also had ADHD (Attention Deficit Hyperkinesis Disorder).

I tried to start a conversation with him. He began playing with me. He was serving me some imaginary delicacies, he prepared then and there, with whatever objects available in the play area. I got ready to relish his preparations. He warned me not to move from my place. He switched on the TV and told me, there were cockroaches all around if I moved from my place. We both enjoyed our tasks, him serving me the food, and instructing me repeatedly and I enjoying the food he had prepared for me. Satisfaction was spilling out from his face. Most of his words I understood by his actions and expressions.

He was sent out with his father and I began talking to his mother. It was a tough task to understand her too. She had too many things to say and was unable to sort them out to prioritise. I sorted out the subjects of discussion for her and requested her to talk only on those areas, till I changed to the next one. Finally, she was able to make a few things clear to me.

She was facing her own problems and they were endless. What I understood about the child was: He was made to watch TV, in anticipation of learning to speak fast, in terms of time. His mother tongue was Tulu and the channels he was exposed to were English ones. He was fussy in his eating habits. So, his eating time was also in front of the TV. He was not allowed to move as the mother feared she would not be able to bring him back and feed him. Instead, he was made to sit on a high table and was told that there were cockroaches all around on the ground. Thus, the child was stuck to one place, not looking anywhere else, other than the TV screen, where there were no cockroaches as he was afraid of them.

There were two main things for me to implement.

The first one was to get rid of the TV time for the child; and the second one was to bring the mother out of her uncontrollable anxiety.

It took a great amount of time and energy on both sides to get the tasks executed. But, the first effective thing was bringing the child out of his TV-screen watching habit. Both mother and son were told to go to a nearby park daily without fail. They both began to enjoy doing it; of course, it was the child more than the mother, who wanted to be there for a longer time. It brought in a lot of changes in the child. This in turn brought down the mother's anxiety.

Now the child is 7 years old, talking, singing, playing and taking part in many of his school activities. He is happily engaged in conversations with his parents and friends.

Contributed by KG Rajalakshmi

Suspect Diagnosis of Autism
Case 2

There was a preschooler brought to the centre by internet savvy parents, after consulting counsellors and psychologists of limited experience with ASD children, who gave the child an ASD diagnosis. This is a dangerous trend of over-diagnosis.

These children were wired children, who imitated what they saw on the screens, be it accent, words, or repetition of words or even odd behaviours. In real time, these appear like 'echolalia' with the child repeating the word an adult or another child uttered or persevering with the same words or behaviour. Basically, these different speech patterns may resemble autistic pattern of communication.

I always ask whether the child was affectionate, even clingy and was sensitive to facial expression of parents, sibling and other children. If a child is capable of emotional bonding with the mother. Emotional bonding and sensitivity to others' emotions is a definite clue that the child is not autistic. I have witnessed a cartoon-induced repeating of words spoken, and constant whining in a preschooler which could be labeled 'echolalia'!

Diagnosis of ADHD

We also get many preschoolers with the complaints of over-activity. Teachers observe overactivity in children. Quite often, parents do not think the child is overactive.

When a child comes in with complaints of over-activity, impulsivity and attention deficit, if we discover it is screen related, we suggest complete denial of screen time. The associated difficult behaviour is attended to in real time, when we have 3 to 4 preschoolers playing together with conventional toys. Even if they are not being cooperative initially, we soon find them playing cooperatively, being helpful, kind to younger or more disturbed children. We find common play is most productive in terms of improvement in the preschool age.

Children who were shy and almost mute, gradually open up and those who were aggressive learn to control anger. To promote healthy behaviour in preschool small groups, especially with ADHD children, stringing beads, sorting out grains, cancelling colours or numbers, help them to persist in tasks, in contrast to what they would normally do. We often make 3 or 4 of them share a large KG cardboard and draw over it with crayons. But each child is given one quarter of the space which belongs to him.

I demand my share!
Case 3

It was a year ago. An elderly man had requested me to help Ananth, his grandson, aged three and half. I met the boy and his father in a park, near the children's area. The boy was allowed to play around the place we sat.

The complaints from the father were:

- He cannot be in one place – he is restless.
- He doesn't listen to anyone, other than his paternal grandmother – sometimes, that too only in some extent, when others are not around.
- He is aggressive verbally and physically, violent most of the times.
- He gets irritated very easily, even without any specific reason.
- He is not at all empathic to anything that happens to anyone, even within the family, except his grandmother – though very rarely.
- While indulging in abusing, he cannot differentiate between an elderly person or a kid of his age, as expected in Indian traditional homes.
- He demands something new continuously.
- These complaints were reported from his school as well.

I went through the details of his daily regular routine activities and also the activities of the people around him.

At home he lived with his parents and paternal grandparents. Grandfather was retired and stayed at home and grandmother took care of the household, as her son and daughter-in-law went out to work in their respective offices. The child went to a playschool from 9.30 am to 12.30 pm. He did not want to go there. After returning home, he played all day with the mobile.

His parents had different time schedules. Mother left home by 10.30 am and returned at 6.30 pm. She was a teacher. She took tuitions at home after her school time. She finished her tuitions by 8.30 pm and by then, she was totally exhausted. She had to attend to some of the kitchen chores to justify her presence in the household, she said.

Father left home around 3 pm and returned at 11.30 pm. He was a programmer and he had to do some of his work at home. So, he was in front of his computer, when the child returned from school and saw the father.

Being a retired person, the grandfather normally went for an early morning walk, read newspaper and watched TV. The grandmother was not an efficient gadget user. She engaged the child with plants, animals and people around the area, in and out of the house. He enjoyed being with her, until he came in contact with the mobile, his most- of- the- time companion.

The father was made to see the whole view from the child's position, as an outsider. The child was restless, irritable, and violent, all because of the exposure of the virtual world during most of his waking hours. He did not have any enjoyable activity to perform, anyone to play with or anyone whom he could talk to, except his grandmother. He was punished for the behaviour, which he had effortlessly learnt through the gadget and he was unable to know the reason. All his behaviours were learnt through what all he watched, through his gadgets, which were very much real to him. He was totally frustrated, disturbed, agitated and confused.

While I was getting the information and educating the father about the situation the child was undergoing, the child was exhibiting his frustrations, disturbances, etc., by repeatedly calling his father, throwing mud all around and upon himself, using bad words to his father and me. When the mother joined us, the father went to the child. Then he was seen playing happily. Mother also was counselled, we explained to her the agony, loneliness and helplessness experienced by the child.

It was not easy for the parents to cut down the mobile time, as it was the child's full-time companion. But they were convinced that it was a short-term hard work to get a long-term result. The father got ready to spend quality time with the child after his playschool time, till he left for his work. Mother got ready to make some other arrangements for her home tuitions and make herself available to the child after her school timings.

After a week, when the father called, he said that he had realised the effect of decreasing the gadget usage of the child (though a gradual process, still an on-going one by then) and also spending quality time with one's own child. This had the approval of the mother too!

Contributed by KG Rajalakshmi

'Time Out' for Disruptive Behaviours

With temper tantrums and aggressive behaviours – the usual behavioural method of 'time out' is used. But it is always one minute per year, for age of the child. If the child is two years old, she gets two minutes of time out. She can stand facing the wall or stand in a corner where she cannot see others. Basically, it means do not pay attention to the tantrum behaviour. An older child gets longer time out. We always make a point of explaining to the child what kind of specific behaviours are targeted for the time out. Of course, praise, a smile and gifts go a long way when pro-social behaviour is displayed.

We also try some of the traditional Indian methods of relaxation for the mind and the body. Simple examples are head massage with amla oil, body massage, avoiding junk food and insist on home cooked traditional meals. Some parents were encouraged to make children follow simple religious rituals. Mealtime with family without the gadgets is encouraged.

We are trying to completely ban screen time with preschoolers. Parents do get convinced, once they notice improvement in their children.

On a Train Journey

Case 4

For more than the past two years, I happened to be a regular weekend commuter between Mysuru and Bengaluru. Each trip has its own charm. I thought of sharing here some glimpses of one of my recent trips.

I had got into an early morning train to Bengaluru, on a Saturday. After I settled there in a comfortable window side seat, a young couple with a cute little girl boarded and settled in the seat in front of me. I normally carry a book, as a food for my journey. Whenever I have a child nearby, I do not take my book out of my bag. My hands were automatically stopped from taking the book out of my bag. I thrust my mobile into my purse.

I looked at the child. She was warmly covered, as it was a chilly early morning after a heavy shower throughout the night. A pretty bundle of curiosity, she sat with her face tucked into her palms. I was enjoying the lovely pose before me. I tried to make contact with her. Tried to talk to her and got her answer in a very feeble voice. I knew I was a stranger to her. I noticed her parents, as there was no sound from either of them.

They both were engaged with their respective mobiles. I looked at the child. I had seen children fighting for their shares of mobiles, whenever such a situation occurred earlier. She asked for neither their mobiles nor their attention. She sat there peacefully. On a cold early morning, she might have woken up early, to have all her early morning tasks, including a bath, to get ready for a train trip to Bengaluru. I assumed she was warming herself up. I thought of helping her to warm up. I continued to interact with her. This time I received a beautiful smile.

We both got into conversation, as the train began to move. There were various things for us to talk about. Of the trains standing, engines moving, people on the platforms, inside the trains, buildings visible on either side, dogs, cows, tiny cockroaches peeping from somewhere, trees, birds, fields, flowers, water drops on the window bars, water flowing in canals, river, stagnant water in the fields, the colours around, the rails, blackened stones in the middle of the two parallel rails, and so on and so forth. We got too busy to seek out anything else. I observed her parents. They were still on their mobiles. There were very little conversations between them and they too were only about the mobile and its outputs.

By the time we reached Srirangapatna, the child was friendly and had found a friend and a playmate in me. We played many games – which may be nonsensical from the viewpoints of any adult – all were enjoyable for both of us. The train reached Mandya, another station, nearly an hour from Mysuru. Her parents were busy with their mobiles. They bought their breakfast from the vendor on the train. The little girl, three years seven months young, a preschooler, we shall name her Dhaatri, wanted Maddur Vada. Her parents bought idli-chutney for breakfast; the girl took one Vada she wanted to eat. She handed it over to me to hold, refusing her mother's offer to hold it for her. Mother fed idli to Dhaatri and Dhaatri wanted me to make the Maddur Vada into smaller pieces so that she could eat them herself.

After her breakfast, she refused to go with her mother to wash her hands. She took me as her escort to the doorside tap, washbasin. She cleaned herself, with my help, and we returned to our seats, to continue with our play and chat.

The father looked at me with wonder and smiled. 'She has made friends with you', he said. I smiled back. I introduced myself and told him that I was very fond of children. I also told him that I worked with children and there I normally educated the parents of the harms of over usage of mobiles by the children and the adults, in the presence of children.

I asked him, 'Doesn't she need your attention? Just imagine after 12-13 years, she will sit with her mobile in her hand and not look at you or hear your words, how would you feel?' Shyly he said, 'We do not use much of mobile at home'. I asked him, 'Do you think she does not need to be attended to when you come out?' He nodded. I continued, 'Children learn more from observing us and copying our words and actions. Did you notice that I had put my mobile inside my purse, as I saw a child in front of me?'

Father was sitting in front of me, the mother beside me and the child on my lap. I assume the father understood my intention. He closed his mobile and put it aside. He retained it almost till the end of the journey. The mother seemed not bothered. She continued with her mobile, and the child continuously played with me.

Dhaatri had carried a lollipop for her dessert. We continued our conversation and plays, while she had her dessert. When she finished it, both our hands had become sticky. This time also, she wanted me to be with her for her cleaning. We had crossed Bidadi and the train was about to reach Kengeri. At this point, the mother might have got the message, I am not sure. She made her hands free of the gadget and began talking to the child. She took her on her lap, cuddled and cajoled her. Both looked very happy.

Contributed by KG Rajalakshmi

It is the responsibility of the parents to encourage strong attachment with their children, parents and siblings. The grandparents can equally enhance this bonding by playing, telling stories, eating meals together or going outdoors. Even watching a good movie together and discussing at their level is useful.

Children learn by imitation, but children learn better from real interaction than from screens. This 'video deficit' appears to last till 30 months. This is all the more important, it is the real people around the toddler who need to provide role models for their healthy behaviours. Better understanding of others' emotions occurs around this time, which is all the more essential to replace screen-time people and objects with real-time people and objects.

Interventions for 4 to 11 Years

IN THIS stage of continuing brain development, it is essential to provide a child impetus of rapid growth in all the domains, physical, intellectual, language, emotional, social, moral and sexual development. The toddler being 'A Scientist in the Crib' in the earlier stage, now becomes more active and independent. From close bonding with the mother or family, the children prefer to move into new relationships with other children initially and with schoolmates upon entering the school. There are dramatic changes in this phase as well.

The child develops new bonds and attachments. The core of all domains of development continues to be play. Real time play promotes overall development, physical development, through acquiring fine and gross motor skills, eye-hand coordination, tactile and kinesthetic stimulation, especially the traditional play, such as hopscotch, ball games, skipping, running race, spinning tops and climbing trees. *I have recorded 53 games played by children in rural schools. We have a veritable storehouse of traditional stories, songs and games in India across the nation. These can indeed form the basis of intervention.*

Cognitive development occurs in the Piagetian framework of development of logic in the pre-operational stage. The logic of pre-operational stage from 11 years, this means what they see in TRAP (TV, Radio and Paper) or interactive screen time is understood differently than a younger child. Below this age, information processing is very different than that of adults. As explained in earlier chapters, the same content may be understood differently by a child, adolescent and an adult.

Language development is most rapid before 10 years of age. Spoken, heard and read out language are absorbed very rapidly as the child's brain is prewired for language acquisition at birth. Children in India are naturally exposed to three or four languages. So, the question whether they should learn only one language, namely English or mother tongue, is of no consequence. They can learn at least 3 to 4 languages of their choice or use before 10 years of age. But the method has to be of 'top down' and not 'bottom up'. No written script should be used, based on conventional school practices. The key is reciprocal communication without involving writing in the earlier years.

Doors to reading open if the stories are read to them, while their eyes follow the moving fingers below the sentences being read. The scripts in Indian languages are numerous and all indigenous languages are phonetic. Once the fine and gross motor skills are achieved through play, writing no longer remains a challenge. The joy of reading should be achieved first. Once the child can read and understand the story line, he may gradually want to write as well as self-challenge, than being forced. Encouraging a child to learn multiple languages is essential as each language carries its own cultural heritage.

This, in addition, accelerates cognitive development.

In the realms of emotional and social development, attachment, empathy and pro-social behaviour are to be encouraged actively. This is something totally derailed by screen time content. Old time stories for children like Mr Rogers or Pollyanna provided healthy content. But the advent of *Angry Birds* has led to the cult of violence. Aggressions need to be replaced by empathy. Pro-social behaviour needs empathy and self-control. Role models are hard to come by in the various tech gadgets.

Robinson et al. in a six-month study, to reduce media use in 8 to 9 years old, adopted a three-step approach of a self-monitoring video usage:

(a) challenged to
(b) turn off screen time for 10 days
(c) a budget of seven hours a week for videos and games.

This would work very well in adolescents. In the study group, peers observed reduced aggression and increased pro-social behaviour. Onus of self or peer monitoring can replace parental monitoring and can be equally effective.

Preferred Effects	**Negative Effects**
Components of	
Pro-social Behaviour	**Antisocial Behaviour**
• Empathy • Compassion • Trust • Ethics The goal is to live in harmony with oneself, family, friends and community	• Mimic aggression in reality • Enjoy aggression in screen time • Content of visual media is to titillate and get the child hooked on anti-social behaviours Evil Gets Rewarded with Power and Money

Can Technology be Ethical, Compassionate and Altruistic?

Problems of Tech in Classrooms

Sometimes, children have a glazed look and appear to be in a trance. When questions were asked about what he was doing, a boy said that he could not get play station out of the head. The intervention? Go back to good old reading of books.

In a study of 1,600 video games in the UK, Griffins and Gortari (2014) reported symptoms of involuntary sensations, thoughts and action, reflexes being experienced by study subjects during video games, even after hours or days after stopping the game. This is called GTP (Game Transfer Phenomenon). Some gamers cannot stop thinking of the games while others display confusion between virtual world and reality. Definitely, one could diagnose this as genuine Obsessive-Compulsive Disorder (OCD).

These symptoms may also be confused with actual psychoses in teenagers. There is a need to check psychotic symptoms, if there is a history of gaming addiction.

In 2011, Tel Aviv University first documented a case of internet related psychoses with even dissociative phenomenon being reported.

In my earlier decades of clinical practice, I have seen very large number of cases of trances and multiple dissociative episodes, including 'mass hysteria'. I wonder if these symptoms are modern version of dissociative spells. One way to check, would be to find out if the symptoms disappear with the 'psychological stress' . This is how we found out the actual reasons and managed our cases to complete recovery.

Would the present-day dissociative symptoms disappear if there is complete unplugging? A study has looked at 114 video-gamer boys and 126 girls and reported that gaming compromised verbal intelligence.

Some Case Illustrations

Case 5

Chethan was six years old when his parents contacted our Child Guidance Centre for counselling. The parents were concerned that the child did not sit in one place, had lack of concentration and did not like writing and was slow in writing. The first session with the child helped identify his addiction to television, continuously watching cartoons.

This made us understand how an entertainment box can badly affect a human being. The cartoon addiction changed Chethan's local accent into American English. The child found it difficult to converse in Kannada and other children found it difficult to understand his accent. This ultimately made him have no friends.

Cure started off by first asking the parents to stop him from watching television altogether. This was a huge step as the child did not have a day when he did not watch TV. But the parents made sure that nobody at their house watched TV.

This step had numerous advantages, the parents were asked to take him to a park and play with him. The child found this as something new and enjoyed playing outdoors.

With this step, the parents were asked to talk in their local languages which were Tamil and Kannada. The child, being of 6 years, learnt his parents' way of talking and this helped him develop the local accent too.

A child can only be motivated to try something new when they are rewarded. Chethan was given a star chart. He was given a star for every new activity he did. The result seen within five sessions was positive. The child was very happy and enthusiastic to play outside. He was taking initiative to talk to people outside as well as in the counselling centre. This showed that, what looked originally like fun and a great past time of TV viewing, had cut off the child's relation with reality and also ruined his basic abilities of talking in local languages.

Contributed by Nisha Shah

Screen Addiction in Five-Year-Old and Management

Case 6

Screen addiction is often discussed as a difficult challenge to deal with. Generally, children are told not to be on screen but not given the alternative means to keep them occupied in their free time.

This example tells us about the importance of the alternatives that we provide.

Nishanth was a 5 year old child brought for counselling by his mother. He was too much addicted to TV and got agitated if made to move away from the TV. He watched TV for a long time, without even taking toilet breaks.

When we talked to the child, the child admitted that he watched TV for long hours and was not ready to stop or reduce it. He said, he did not have anything else to do in his free time as there were no siblings or friends nearby. Parents were scared to allow him to play outside as they lived on a busy road. So, he started watching TV whenever he felt bored and gradually that became a habit and he got addicted to it.

As there were few options in his case, we had to look for what was possible. We asked him about his interests and hobbies. Based on them, a few activities like drawing, colouring and indoor games were suggested. He was happy to do drawing and colouring but wanted someone to play with him.

We found that his grandmother stayed with them. She was not in a position to do much of physical movements, but loved to spend time with him.

So, Nishanth was encouraged to learn some new games from his grandmother and play with her. Within a few days, he learnt some board games and started playing with his grandmother. Gradually, he started inviting other family members also to join in his games. Like this, his TV time came down gradually and reached a stage where he did not get agitated if he was not getting to watch TV. Later, his mother reported that, he was showing interest in other activities, academics and appeared to be more cheerful.

Contributed by Sindhu HR

Late Night TV Watching
Case 7

Dhanya was in 3rd standard, studying in an English medium school when I first met her. She was 8 years 7 months old, a single child and from a middle-class family. Her father worked in a weaving factory and the mother was a housewife. Both the parents were educated up to 10th Std.

She was brought with complaints of her incomplete class notes and forgetfulness about school lessons, a complaint persistent for two years, i.e. from 1st standard. In the present year, the school said, she slept in class. Bed wetting was another major complaint.

While interacting with the mother, I got to know that the child watched television till late night. Since the mother had health issues, Dhanya was left to watch television. This impacted her academics also. Dhanya ate more frequently and began to put on weight. She also got angry, fought with others and did not listen to parents. She hit her mother and threw tantrums. She refused to go to school.

After few sessions of counselling, the child began to play with friends after school, and joined a dance class as she was very much interested in dance. Even the mother stopped watching TV and began spending time with Dhanya after school. Their TV time came down and the child began going to sleep early.

It's Dinner Time – no TV!

Case 8

Madhav was a boy of 10 years 7 months, studying in 5th standard in a CBSE school. He had a sister who was 6 years old. He was from a middle-class family. His parent had completed SSLC (10th grade).

He was weak in academics, spent a lot of time watching TV and played games on the mobile. He got angry, became arrogant, when asked to do schoolwork. He lived in a joint family and had multiple caretakers like grandparents, uncles and aunts.

During his counselling sessions, his parents and family were made aware of the bad effects of watching television and mobile games on children. He was told to play with friends and to get into a sports coaching class which he was very much interested in. The family was advised to have family time during dinner without television on.

After a few sessions, Madhav looked cheerful and expressed his difficulties in academics and these the teachers took care of through remedial work and he improved in studies.

Contributed by Veena Suresh

Interventions for 11 Years and Above

ADOLESCENCE IS a special phase where there is growth spurt and much variations in their physiological and psychological growth profile. They believe that they are grown-ups while parents and teachers believe that they are still children and should obey them and be guided by them. On the other hand, there are family conflicts arising in the areas of discipline, relations to siblings, victimisation, criticism, immaturity, rebellion and lack of supervision. Age-related psychological problems of sexuality, school dropout, antisocial and aggressive behaviour, at times even psychotic breakdowns occur during this phase. IoT interactive technology is, particularly for the very young and adolescents, very critical as they both are very vulnerable groups.

In China, internet addiction is the number one health crisis, with over 20 million internet addicted teens. South Korea has opened 400 tech addiction rehabilitation centres. In the USA the use of technology is promoted by the industry and schools too are pushing for it. Let India not go their way.

Some of the following research studies throw light on some intervention possibilities.

Nature Adventure Camps as Intervention

This detailed account is to provide the reader with details that can be incorporated in all our outdoor nature activities that we advise our parents. Pali Institute is a typical outdoor overnight camp outside Los Angles, which has a description that is worth emulation, where no electronic devices are permitted. It is worth emulating, irrespective of country.

Students hike through the forest to explore and learn about the ecosystems around them. They identify flora and fauna and participate in hands-on activities. Through these various activities, students understand the history of the forest as the ecosystems come alive before their eyes.

Outdoor Skills: Mixing nature's beauty with outdoor survival, students learn the Ten Essentials for any outdoor trip. They learn fire-building and cooking food in an outdoor setting. While in the forest, they will band together as a team to build emergency shelters.

Animal Survivor: Students are taught the importance and dynamics of food chains/webs and how species depend on one another for survival. In a fast-paced activity, students are assigned an identity: carnivores, herbivores or omnivores. They must search for food while avoiding predators (their peers). Each student begins the game with a certain number of lives and must have at least one life remaining at the end to be a 'survivor'.

Day Hike: Schools have the opportunity to select their focus for a hike, such as bird watching, visiting a nature center and greenhouse, or shortened versions of a double-session forest ecology or outdoor skills class.

Archery: Students learn the history and mechanics of archery, one of the oldest arts and means for survival. They are introduced to the basic physics of a bow and arrow, as well as the proper handling of this ancient device. With this knowledge, they participate in target shooting. Students gain an understanding of the importance of archery and its influence on society.

Orienting: Students find their sense of direction while engaging in one of several orienteering courses. During the expedition, they learn how to navigate through the forest by using compasses and coordinates. They gain an understanding of the various skills involved in planning travel from point A to point B.

An example from India on growing up with the wilderness would be conservationist Kenneth Anderson's way of bringing up his son Don (as Don explains in his own autobiography), of walking through forests, knowing to differentiate wild monkey chatter and a panicked monkey chatter, knowing the flowers and the insects, and the bees and the dungs and the trails, all crossed on foot, learning the sounds and smells of the forests. No phones in these forests until 2000.

While for centuries, the main method for social learning for humans has been face to face communication, it was with the advent of the 21st century, that digital media has become a widely used method of communication. It precludes eye contact, understanding body language and gestures along with emotional bonding of deeper and lasting kind.

A study by Uhis Yalda et al (2014) used the above Pali model with two groups of school children. In this study, 51 children were the experimental group of 6th graders. They were exposed to exclusive opportunities and experiences, outdoor activities and social interventions with absolutely no access to regular screen time. The outdoor camp was educational, where the students immersed in outdoor activities to enhance understanding of science, cooperative living, fending for themselves and so on. The children who were away from screens for five days improved significantly in reading facial expression when they had person to person interaction, absence of screen time, real time engagement with others and nature enhanced understanding emotion.

This example can be used as an intervention for screen immersion.

A control group of 54 of their classmates in the school had their on-screen activities. Participants in the control group attended school, with a typical week of instruction at a California public elementary school (i.e. history, English, math instruction, etc.) each day between the pre- and post-test, with no restrictions placed on their media use by the research team.

Both groups were tested before and after the five-day experiment. While the researchers did not collect information about after school, beyond asking children about their typical day's media activities, a teacher at the school polled her class and told the researchers that the majority of the children participate in sports two to four times a week.

In India, wherever one goes today, be it on a train, bus, park or a family dinner, one comes across group of youngsters, each one with one's own device. They disregard even natural safety concerns of cliff edge, riverbank or ocean while 'selfies' are taken with total disregard for the environment. Even normal risk-taking behaviour takes a toll, for example when two teenaged girls stood on the railway tracks in a small town, to take selfies of themselves with an oncoming train. One died on the spot and the other died in a hospital, nearly every bone broken. Perhaps training in survival should be a must before selfies kill a large number of children.

In India, in tech cities like Bangalore, which is called the Silicon Valley of India, the BEASTS are roaming free, devouring our teenagers. The monsters they are fighting in virtual reality have already overpowered and swallowed them. India needs to do soul searching towards the damage wreaked by them. There should be tech rehabilitation centres as corporate responsibility.

Game induced psychosis: A tech-driven teenager shows altered behaviour of psychotic prospective, with glazed look, unkept and indifferent. In fact, he does not even know where he is as he continues to see what he sees in virtual reality in the reality itself. This occurs when there is excessive gaming, sleep deprivation and loss of appetite. The child is 10 to 12 hours of a day in one such state, as if it were a world of war. Here we are dealing with a digital drug and even when unplugged, the teenager is totally disoriented to time, place and person as in the case of psychoses.

What is the attraction (compulsion) of placing all information about oneself for better or worse on the public domain? In early part of my career, I studied three groups: psychotics, neurotics and well-adjusted youth on the sentence completion test. While psychotics displayed bizarre ideation, the well-adjusted gave brief and positive responses. Neurotics on the other hand, filled all the available space with their painful, tedious self-disclosures. Neurotics had a great need to unburden themselves by uncensored self-disclosure.

I wonder, if the compulsion to self-disclosure is the cause of the negative content of online communication in the social media. In medical terms, one would clearly call it a neurotic behaviour.

According to Karadaras (2016), these teenagers are looking for a sense of purpose and share this purpose with other gamers. The other reason is 'escapism' where the teenager feels he is a misfit. While others use drugs or alcohol, these youngsters use fantasy itself. Often, these children may come from dysfunctional families. At times, the conflicts may be internal as well. Here predisposition by temperament plays a major role as well. Could these be one of the reasons for higher suicide rates?

While alcohol or drugs are not socially approved, tech addiction is less recognised, noted or shunned by society. It is the invisible enemy. Fantasy in reality promotes imagination and creativity. As pointed out by Negroponte of MIT media, while iconic, the so-called educational games like *Oregon Trail* leaves very little to imagination by contrast.

In the virtual world, all possible images in their violent manifestations do not give any scope to imagination. Word sparks images and evokes metaphors. When you read a novel, much of the colour, sound and motion come from within one's fantasy. In the new video classrooms, our kids get entertainment and over-stimulation while learning becomes optional.

Perhaps a meta-analysis of all successful interventions of individual cases or in groups by institutions will offer insights to this new area of mental health, so that we have guidelines not only for assessment but also for effective intervention. However, it is clear that the approach should be holistic, consisting of developmental stage, sociocultural, economic, ethnic, apart from time, content of the screen exposure etc. The main effort should be eliminating screen time for the very young and set limit to the older children.

Dr Doan's analogy is a metaphor I find very easy to follow and communicate to the parents.

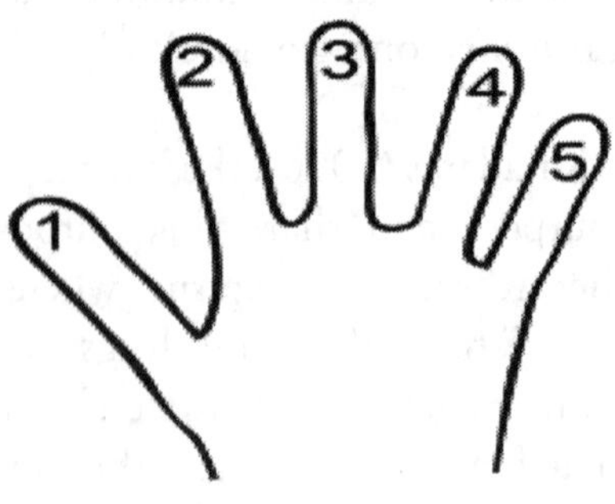

1. Analytical ability, eye-hand coordination and quick reflexes technology benefits.

2. Communication skills (verbal and non-verbal).
3. Recognise emotions in self (empathy) and others.
4. Social bonding and family.
5. Self-control.

If one is all thumbs, you will be totally dysfunctional. You need all the five fingers for your wellbeing. This metaphor leads to easy explanations to parents and children.

Though Teenagers' violent behaviour relation to screen is well-established, there are a large number of studies that deny gadgets can be harmful. Adolescent girls use less of video games in general, and rarely use games with violence. They also react adversely to violent content. This may render them less at risk for over aggression. Thus, countering aggression induced by gaming and video content is to be done by shifting from virtual world to real world activities.

Nature of Happy and Pro-social Adolescents

- Attachment to parents and siblings, peers, teachers and other adults.
- Limit setting to screen time and enhanced real-life interactions and activities.
- Promotion of empathy, attachment and pro-social behaviour, based on real time activities.
- The above are as important as cognitive development which will occur simultaneously with the overall development.

Unfit to be a Friend

Case 9

Priya was in 7th standard when one evening, when she went out to play with her classmates/friends who lived close to her house, they started talking about looks and discussing who was of the right height/weight/looks etc.

Priya was the youngest of the group, who loved to play

different sports. She was what everyone called a tomboy. She was petite with short hair, sparkly eyes and a sweet smile. The other girls were older, some of them had reached menarche and were showing curves on their bodies. Priya was not too keen to talk about this topic, she decided to ditch the conversation and headed out to play with the boys.

After a while when she came back, everyone in the girl group teased her for trying to be a boy. She was called gay and a boy and few other things which confused her at first. When the girls started laughing, she was hurt. She hurried home only to find out that her father had fallen sick and her mother had rushed him to the hospital. They were suspecting that her father had a heart attack. Her older sister was busy with her studies as she was in the 10th standard. She was too busy with her homework and studies to have observed the changes in Priya.

Four days passed before her mother and father came back home from the hospital. Her mother was extremely anxious and worried about her husband's health. They were busy with the medical follow ups and other things and did not worry too much about their little girl, as Priya was always out-going, independent and social. They had lived in the same house for more than 5 years now and Priya knew most of the neighbours.

During the time her father was in the hospital, her parents had given both the girls a smart phone so they could call the mother when they went to their grandparent's house or came back home. Priya was seen using the phone to browse the internet and her parents assumed that she was using it to help her with her homework. They also noticed that she was not going out to play but since it was just a month before the annual exam, they decided not to bother pushing her out to play and let her focus on her revision of her lessons.

Over the months, Priya completely stopped going out. She refused to come out of her room when they had guests visiting and refused to go to school. Few months passed and summer holidays were over, Priya began her 8th standard class.

She attended the school the first day, saw all her friends who started making fun of her again. From that day onwards she refused to go to school. Priya had not discussed the name-calling and bullying by her friends with anyone – neither with her sister nor her mother. When she refused to go to school for weeks, her mother got worried and called me. I have known them personally for many years and I asked Priya's mother to bring her for counselling so that we can know the cause of her behaviour.

Priya refused to get out of the house. She would be constantly on the phone, locked in the room. Her mother did not know if she was chatting with someone or playing a game or whatever that she was doing on the phone. When the parents tried to take away her phone or talk to her about the consequences of being on the phone for long time, she would scream at the top of her voice, cry and make a big scene. Her parents, being mild and simple, gave in to her demands rather than have such drama in the house every day.

Priya would lock herself in the room, be with the phone all day and night. Her mother wo ld leave her a plate of food, milk and snacks in front of the room door and she would see the empty plate after many hours or the next day. Since the room had an attached bathroom, they had no clue if she ate anything or flushed it down the toilet. Priya would come out for a few minutes and if anyone asked her any question, she would go lock herself in the room or throw a huge tantrum, screaming and crying.

She would not eat, she cut her hair in the front which would cover her entire face, made her mother buy a wide frame glasses which covered most of her face, wear only baggy sweatshirts and loose track pants. Her parents were at their wits end, trying to talk to her and unable to understand what was happening.

About 15 months after the first incident, Priya fell very sick. She had to be taken to a doctor. They took her to an adolescent and paediatric doctor, as she refused to see their family doctor. When the new doctor asked her to remove her baggy outfits, her parents were shocked to see how much weight she had lost. She had to be taken for immediate psychiatric care and counselling.

After the counsellor was successful in building the rapport and talk to Priya, the family found out that her friends had continued to make comments on her looks in a very subtle way and Priya became more and more conscious about her body. She started dreading meeting people who would invariably make some comment about how much she had grown/not grown, her hair or height and her choice of outfit.

She chose to sit in her room and chat with one of her schoolmates who used to listen to her and give her tips as to how to lose weight. He was not a friend that anyone knew much about. But he was her friend, who understood her and she preferred texting with him all the time than go out and actually talk to people.

Priya was diagnosed with severe eating disorder, social anxiety, depression and it was compounded by mobile addiction. After three years of therapy and counseling, Priya was able finish her high school with some difficulty and moved to pre-university college.

Contributed by Anitha Sudhir

•

Will You Be My Friend?

Case 10

Thirteen year old Anand's mother complained of his poor academic performance and incomplete notes and that he played video games on computer and watched rap music on YouTube for long hours. His mother was anxious and worried about his school performance and about his wasting too much time on computer. He was in 9th standard.

Anand was a very quiet boy. During interactions, he said mother was strict and not allowing him to play with friends. Even his elder brother was busy with studies and did not interact with him much. Slowly he got into the habit of watching music on You tube and began to learn a few rap songs. This became a habit and he also enjoyed playing video games. Video games were the common topic of discussion among his peer group.

During counseling session, parents were told about the importance of outdoor games. His brother was also told to spend some quality time with Anand, like going out on weekends and have a good time together. Thereafter, Anand was able to manage his computer time and study time. Even his mother felt better.

It is My Show Time

Case 11

Padma, a 12-year old studying in 7th standard, had come with a strange complaint. She had done a video recording in her aunt's mobile about how the first night would be after marriage, both audio and video, exposing her own body.

The parents were shocked when they found this out and did not know how to go further with this. She had gone to paternal uncle's house and was alone there. She took her aunt's mobile and shot this video. Later, the aunt saw it and showed it to her mother. The mother was angry and hit the girl. But the family worried about why she did it.

When she came for counseling, father spoke separately with the counsellor and mentioned the above incident. Initially the rapport with her was built by the counsellor regarding her school, friends and hobbies. Padma was a brave girl and watched a lot of comedy shows. Her interest was to become a TV anchor. She enjoyed performing in front of audience. She was also a fun-loving girl.

Slowly, after a few sessions, the counsellor told her about the effects of mobile and how all private matters can become public if one is not aware of it. She accepted that she had done something like that, a few days ago. She opened up about the incident and said that one of her friends in the school van had told her about such videos. So, without knowing the consequence, she had shot this video and wanted to watch it and delete it. She had tried to delete it, but the mobile got switched off due to low battery charge. She thought it should be gone and nobody would know about it. But unfortunately, when the aunt had put the mobile on charge, it was not deleted and she watched it and had informed Padma's parents.

Now Padma understood the consequences, and adverse effects of gadgets if not used wisely. Even the parents were given some awareness about smart phones and internet. More such awareness programmes to parents about internet and smart phones need to be given to parents of young people.

Contributed by Veena Suresh

Guidelines to Parents

NEW YORK TIMES offers a guideline on how to limit kids' tech use (Melanie Pinola). This is applicable globally as digital technology's reach is global. We in India – parents, teachers, healthcare providers, policy makers and administrators – are equally culprits in the gadget-addiction the next generation is becoming addicted to rapidly. As this book is being written, we have to take into account, a threat like a global viral attack and long periods of lockdowns where phones and television are the only two gadgets keeping people home. At such a time, it is challenging to say, be careful of digital technology. Nevertheless, we say it, because one should not forget Frankenstien's Monster. Digital gadgets, AI, IoT, mobile telephones, television, online games, play stations – we recommend extreme caution when letting children under 19 use these without monitoring.

Technology is here to stay and we cannot wish it away. We are in the midst of a fifteen-year social experiment that no one is controlling, being swallowed by device myth-makers. Thus, misuse and overuse looms over the horizon, says the NYT guideline.

Aim for Balance

- Your parenting is different from those of others. Your family can reap the benefit of technology without its harmful effects.
- Watch out for signs of unhealthy tech usage. The signs are when kids complain of being bored or unhappy – when they cannot access technology, throw tantrums or offer strong resistance when limit setting for screen time is attempted. There is evidence to suggest that screen time interferes with sleep, school performance and face to face communication.
- Healthy or unhealthy tech usage needs to be updated as does technology.
- Assess regularly the quality of your child's digital interaction. All screen times are not equal. For example, is the content appropriate to your child's age? Some applications are thought-provoking and useful while others may be passive and negative in their impact. Look out for privacy settings which aim to protect your child's privacy.

Beware of the Trojan Horse of Advertising

The term Trojan horse applies to the deception practised by the digital industry to compel the parents and children to see and buy their products.

- Set limits to 'on' time activities percentage and 'off' time real activities. That is gadget off time.
- Draw the line when screen is off limits. These may be during mealtimes, in the car while being dropped or

picked up, in the school and whenever the family is physically together.

Be a Role Model

Technology is irresistible even to parents. We too check our phones too often, spend long hours on the internet, not necessarily at work, watch our favourite shows. Quite often, children have to compete for our attention. Nearly half the parents in one study reported technology interfering with interaction with their child three or more times on a typical day. (Imagine how it comes in the way of the parents' interaction among themselves and causing a double whammy for the child seeing parents being inattentive to each other.)

- Set boundaries for work time and family time.
- Time to unplug and talk face to face.
- Picking up and dropping children.
- School activities.
- Coming home from work, both parents and children should reconnect in real time during meals, dining out or visiting outdoors park or zoo. This is ideal time to talk.
- Decide when you are really busy and need to be plugged in.

American Paediatric Association 2016 Guidelines:

Only video chatting with relatives – for those below 18 months, eg. Skyping with grandparents or relatives when they are absent.

Watching together quality programmes such as Sesame Street – for 18 to 24 months.

One to two hours of screen time for 2 to 5 years.

Six years and above – within stipulated limits in a consistent manner.

Right balance needs to be achieved.

- Limit tech to the bare minutes, not hours.

- Do not use educational DVDs. Baby Einstein and the other so-called educational DVDs which are marketed exclusively have been shown to be linked to sleep problems, delays in learning essential skills such as vocabulary. The same rule goes for the use of Alexa for teaching your baby.
- If a programme is good, view together and discuss as well and play together.
- Best kids' applications (Apps) offer curated tests. (But the author strongly objects and believes that applications are no substitute for actual playing or singing with mother, siblings and other children.)

Protect Your Devices

Do not give unlimited access to children without parents being present. This industry offers a lot of tips to parents to buy more applications to benefit the tech industry. The parents are never warned about how they are being trapped by media and product marketing. Some examples could be: Do not text while driving. Avoid oversharing on the media. It is similar to warning signs on cigarette packets.

I would add, it is disrespectful and lack of courtesy if you use your screen when someone is with you and talking to you.

Make tech a family affair and family tech rules. The family discusses, who plays what role such as doing the dishes or taking care of the pet or where to go for a vacation. There can be a family media use policy regarding the decisions like screen-time, who, when, for how long and this can be applied to even entertainment. You could watch a movie together which is enjoyable and that too only during weekends or holidays. Such policies need to be open and consensus-driven, not top down.

- Be involved with your child's tech experiences. By this, you can watch the content accessed. If they are ahead of you, learn from them, share their virtual experiences as far as possible on games like 'minecraft', 'fortnite games', 'teen speak', watch it but critically and discuss with the child as to why it is so attractive.

- Tailor your approach to match the temperament, age and needs of the child. Some babies may 'be soothed' by soft music– as played by the Baby TV channel. Some may become alert to certain sounds during bedtime.

Toddlers and Preschoolers (2 to 5 years)

When your toddler is running and exploring the environment, it is hard to keep the electronic devices out of the way. A survey by Erikson Institute found that 86 per cent of the parents found tech use of their children beneficial including literacy, school readiness and school success. While there are more applications and gadgets, it is recommended that tech use should be made a small slice of their learning and activities pie.

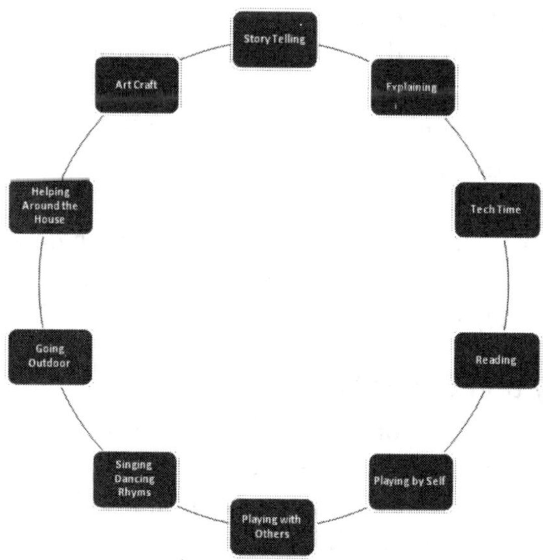

- Can you really make technology use a bonding time (Trojan Horse by tech lobby)?
- Choosing games and applications (Trojan Horse by tech lobby).

Let parents know the content of the above before use by kids, without stating the obvious, that this is not the concern of the manufacturers.

- Set tech-free time and spaces.

Young Children (6 to 12 Years)

It is the right time to set up and reinforce healthy tech habits.

Children in school are likely to have school related work that requires screen time.

Set up child accounts with Microsoft parent controls.

Encourage Creativity

Examples given are Osmo, Scratch, Toontastic, Wipeout, Create and Crash (Trojan Horses – why not do the above activities in real time and space and make them truly creative by being child-centred).

Internet directed activities are monotonous, repetitive, non-creative and adopts top down approach. One may claim graphic art is superior, but all the heads are round, looks are gory and colour combinations are identical, till they are upgraded to new sets of colours. Even creativity is mechanical and automated, when it is carried out in the top down manner by the techno experts. Techies are not necessarily creative, repetitive they surely are.

Privacy and Security Concern

Discuss the safety concerns with children. Even that too has an application FOSI 'online safety cards for kids' technology. (Perhaps using a thorn to remove a thorn!). This is very clearly dealt with in detail by Sebastian Edassery in Chapter 7.

Watch Out for Cyber Bullying

The American clinical psychologist, Lisa Damour, offers the following guidelines:

- Do not be a passive bystander if you witness bullying

online or in real life.

- Alert an adult.
- Stand up to the bully on behalf of the victim.
- Go out of the way to help the victim. (Stop bullying. Government offers advice to parents and children.)
- Their own phone?

Most children in the US get a phone at around 10 years of age or a couple of years earlier, according to a Nielson research. Parents give them phones so that they can keep in touch with them. Pros and cons of this needs to be discussed between the children, parents and teachers. As the context is most important, there cannot be a single solution to this process.

Some Guidelines:

- Are they responsible for their belongings?
- Do they follow rules of their use?
- Can they be trusted to handle the text, photos and videos responsibly?

Most experts recommend that as long as possible kids' exposure to online bullies, child predators, sexting and the distraction of social media should be avoided.

Teens 13 to 18 Years

Adolescents want more freedom and privacy. But they need to be protected and kept safe. Maintain trust and stay connected.

Set Rules

- Never text while driving.
- Never share inappropriate photos or videos.
- Always text to inform when you arrive or leave your destination.
- Best practices
    - Discuss positive and negative aspects of phone use.

- How to identify and ignore marketing messages.
- How to identify false information or fake news.
- Check periodicity, follow your kids on social media.
- Establish trust.
- Spying and monitoring can easily be merged. You need to keep your boundaries clear and respect the privacy of your teenager.
- Steer them into productivity.
- Avoid tech addiction.

As you are a role model to your child, check if you yourself are a screen addict.

David Greenfield of University of Connecticut lists 15 questions for you to assess if you are a screen addict:

1. Do you find yourself spending more time on the phone?
2. Do you mindlessly pass time staring at the phone?
3. Do you lose track of time when on your phone?
4. Do you find yourself spending more time texting, tweeting or emailing than talking to people in person?
5. Has the amount of time you spend on phone been increasing?
6. Do you wish you were less involved with phone?
7. Do you keep your phone turned on under the pillow or next to your bed regularly?
8. Do you find yourself viewing, answering texts and emails at all hours – interrupting what you are doing?
9. Do you use phone while driving?
10. Does it decrease your ability?
11. Are you reluctant to be without your cell phone even for a short time?
12. Do you feel uncomfortable when you leave it behind accidentally?

13. Near your plate on the dining table.
14. When it rings you have intense urge to check?
15. Do you immediately check?

New York Times - Denis Grady

Some suggestions as to how to break up your screen habit:

- Reframe the way you think what is pleasurable.
- What do you want to pay attention to?
- Set yourself for success, read a book, cook.
- Turn social media off.
- Disable notifications.
- No phones during meals.
- Speed bumps.
- Pay attention to your body.
- Practice trial separation from the phone.
- There are time tracking applications such as MOMENT, Ability Time (OFF TIME), Freedom Block, access to problem sites. (Trojan Horse applications to get rid of other applications.)

Curious association between substance abuse and internet addiction in the past one decade has been noticed with decrease in the substance and increase in the internet addiction in the USA.

Drinking, smoking and drug addiction are down, while internet addiction is up. However, the lowered substance abuse may very well be due to extensive efforts towards increasing awareness. Contrary to the above, it is speculated that internet addiction replaces substance by creating similar dopamine increase and excitement. The question is: whether internet addiction is better than substance abuse. While the drug abuse rates are down among the teenagers, suicide rates are up. Also reports of less aggressive and oppositional behaviour is noted in general among the teenagers

To conclude, the general outlines are excellent, but they put the onus of limiting internet use only on the parents for supervision and children for their self-control. But that is only half the problem.

Who regulates the toxic nature of IoT and AI industry, advertisements and the unethical means of reaching out and compelling them to buy the products? Who regulates the companies that provide technology, connectivity and content? Mostly, worldwide, it is governments. Who will control the beast, while we try our best to protect ourselves and our children?

Will they regulate themselves instead of letting the floodgates open without the onus of responsibility and morality.? This is the classic story of an elephant in the room that no one speaks about!

One is very tempted to take up the cudgels like teen age activist Greta Thunberg and ask the Techno Industry and their marketing team .... **How dare you?**

Approaches to Solutions

AS YOU go through this book, you will be bewildered by the complexities of the globalisation of technology and its adverse impact on the young population. At times, metaphors help to simplify complex issues. I would like to use two metaphors, one of Dr Doan and one of mine own.

Doan compares the impact of technology with the metaphor of your left hand that is described in an earlier chapter. The thumb represents positive benefits of technology in speeding up your reaction time and eye hand coordination, reflexes and attention to intricate details on the screen. The index finger represents communication skills, the middle finger represents family and social bonding, the ring finger represents recognising emotions in self and others (empathy) and the little finger represents the most important aspect, namely self-control. If you have only your thumb, you are all thumbs and useless. Think about the implications of this excellent metaphor.

The second metaphor has its roots in my project area where I have worked with thousands of school children in rural and tribal areas in HD Kote in my home State Karnataka.

This forest in the foothills of Western Ghats is famous for the flora and fauna of rain forests and typical of elephant population. Taming and training of elephants for army, essential for the royalty in various parts of India, was a common practice. HD Kote was a fertile ground for developing indigenous ways of capturing, taming and training of wild elephants. There are even today indigenous people who take care of training the elephants called 'Mahouts'.

'Operation Khedda' was the traditional way of capturing elephants in the wild. The tribals would build a strong structure in the model of a mouse trap, with heavy trap doors. Then the tribals would drive the elephants from all the four directions to this khedda (a trap), accompanied by drumbeats and shouting, moving in concentric circles, reducing the circumference slowly, in a graded manner. When close to the khedda structure, the elephants would rush towards the only open gate way and get inside and get trapped. Then 'Mahouts' or the trainers would take over and train them to carry timber logs, for temple services or to be a part of army cavalry.

When we refer to the technology giants, often the common expression is 'Elephant in the Room'. Everybody is affected by its presence, but no one talks about it or does anything about it. The Khedda model can offer us solutions that can be translated into action. For example, acknowledge the presence of elephants, identify the damages done in their rampaging of human habitat, create awareness in the public domain, build pressure groups, finally drive them into submission and contain them and use them for the benefits of human, animal and plant resources and live in harmony with the environment.

Reflections based on research findings in the 1980s and

1990s[7] on how much media exposure do children have, what are the cognitive social outcomes of screen time, its impact, health and safety and what policy initiatives are needed, need to be done at both policy and societal levels.

1. Children's use and access to interactive media
2. Cognitive and social outcomes of interactive media use
3. Health and safety issues
4. Policy concerns.

Most research to date are studies on
(a) Amount of time spent
(b) Influence of violent content in video games
(c) Impact on social behaviour.

However, there has been little research on the impact on children's health issues like seizures, addiction and weight gain/ loss and, how children understand advertising, disclosure and privacy concerns. Influences of, especially, newer technologies such as devices, wireless technology, hand-held and interactive toys/ robots have not been examined and recorded or studied.

Examinations of media convergence such as content across platforms along with media consolidation by mergers too have been lacking.

Media Use and Access

Small-scale and large-scale studies show ownership of computer in the USA from 68 per cent to 70 per cent – 2 per cent growth in 1999-2000.

Ownership of video games from 67 per cent to 81 per cent – 14 per cent growth.

Online access from 41 per cent to 52 per cent – 11 per cent growth.

7 Drawn mainly from Research Compendium, 2002/2004 Wartella et al.

In India

With over 560 million internet users, India is the second largest online market in the world, ranked only behind China. By 2021, there will be over 600 million internet users in India. Despite the large base of internet users, only 34 per cent of the Indian population could access the internet in 2017. Even then, this was a big increase when compared to the previous few years, when the internet penetration rate stood at approximately a little over 10 per cent. At the same time, almost 70 per cent of the internet users in the country were noted to be men, compared to just 30 per cent of female internet users.

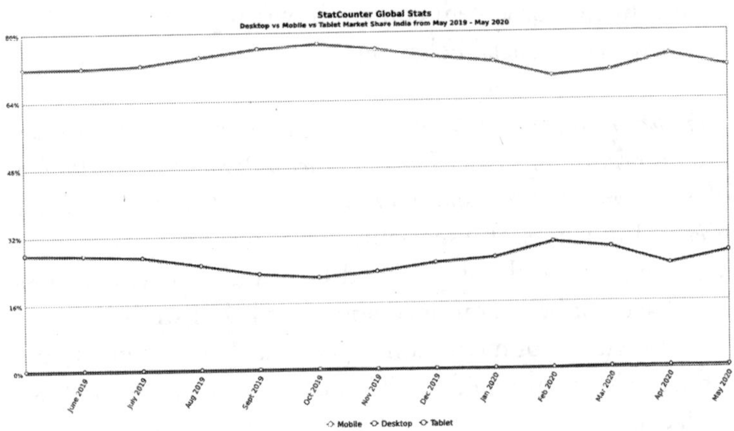

A year-long Canadian study by Jansen, Boyce and Picket (2012) cross-sectionally studied 9,672 sixth to tenth graders and longitudinally studied 1,861 ninth and tenth graders on actual physical fights and bullying. In the former group, the computer and video games used were associated with the screen time violence. In the older children there was increase in real time aggression. It is obvious that it is important to study short term and long term impact of screen time.

Anderson et al (2017), in a meta analysis of a very large number of net-viewing hours, arrived at the following conclusions: The sheer number of hours spent by the youth on the internet, computers and video games has led to policymakers, parents, teachers and researchers alike to question potential negative and positive impact on players. The authors of this study at the outset state that video games are not inherently 'bad'. There are many potential cognitive and social benefits of video game play; some have received empirical support. Well-designed video games are excellent teachers. But violent video games can have negative impact on players.

A vast majority of scholars, paediatricians, and all major scientific panel reports agree: evidence supporting theoretically well-founded hypotheses linking violent media to aggressive and violent behaviour is considerably more voluminous and convincing than the rare contradictory findings. It is then logical to expect that if violence at home, in school and the community can lead to aggressive behaviour in children, it stands to reason even media violence will have similar impact.

There are several risk factors that promote violence and media is not the only single risk factor. But it is a significant one. Other risk factors may occur in a limited contexts of violence at home, school and community, but media violence all too easily becomes pervasive in the world. Major scientific organisations, including the American Academy of Paediatrics, the American Academy of Child and Adolescent Psychiatry, the American Medical Association, the American Psychiatric Association, the American Psychological Association, the US Surgeon General, the Society for the Psychological Study of Social Issues, and the International Society for Research on Aggression, all say so. A comprehensive meta-analysis found that exposure to violent video games **increases** aggressive thoughts, angry feelings, physiologic arousal, hostile appraisals, and aggressive behaviour and **decreases** prosocial behaviour (eg, helping others) and empathy.

In India there are several overviews of international research and a few technologies promoting small-scale studies on this subject. But indepth study of screen time and impact on children is rarely found. There are studies, desinged to promote intervention for ADHD and so on. There are plenty of anecdotal reports in the newspapers and magazines. We can draw some parallels from the Asian studies from Korea and China. *Indian studies need to focus on the diversities and to plan accordingly for different age groups speaking different languages, and with affluent or disadvantaged back backgrounds.* But focus must be on intervention for different age groups for Internet addictions. The approach should be holistic and use multiple techniques that are individually tailored to the needs of child and the family. Intervention in groups at schools can be considered as well.

Age Differences

In the US study, children between 2 to 7 years used more educational games while 9 to 12 years preferred video games. Video game use increased with age. Older children 12 to 14 years used computers more as well as more video games. The world has come 20 years forward after the Wartella study.

Socio-economic Status and Digital Divides

Largescale studies have shown that higher income households were likely to own a computer and have internet access. For example, white Americans own more tech gadgets than African and Hispanic Americans. However, these groups had access to video games even more than higher socio-economic groups. This has significant implications in India where despite high levels of poverty, mobile phones have become ubiquitous.

Parents Education and Ethnicity

A decade ago, access to computer was associated with income of the family, parents' education, ethnicity and parents' work-based experiences with computers. This in turn, allowed the high-income group children to gain greater advantage of computer access, when compared to disadvantaged children.

It is important to know that digital divide is a function of disparities in socio-economic status, education and ethnicity. Disadvantages within the community come in the way of reducing the digital inequality. But when we weigh in the disadvantage of pervasive use of technology, we know that at least a sizable population in India are yet to be swamped by technology. Digital divide needs to be understood as a divide of the mind – rather than of technology or access to it. Perhaps digital divides preserve the brains of young ones, safe from the monster, as the monster can hardly earn from this population. However, this hope is laced with a big question mark as the number of *smartphone* users in India in 2020 is estimated to be about 300 milion. It means – a third of the population do have access, not forgetting that this is a young population and future parents.

Cognitive Development and Learning

Interactive media are rapidly converging, presenting new potential for children's learning. The platforms (computer software, videogame and internet) are less important than influencing activities performed and mass socialisation theories. Some of these interactive technologies have even drawn from classical theories of child development, apart from including its own information processing model.

Cognition

Drawing from Piagetian and Vygotskian models are the components:

a. Situated knowledge (in the psychological, social and cultural context)
b. Computer software as scaffolding
c. Inquiry
d. Dialogue
e. Framing

Vygotsky's Zone of Proximal Development (ZPD) has been used for designing software systems to the benefit of the learner. Of course, individual differences among children are not to be overlooked (Luekin 2001). Children should be provided high quality and quality support but only those children with high and average intellectual ability can actually utilise deep support and below average children are generally found to be poor learners. Providing software alone is not the only necessary condition. These findings tell us that a large number of economically disadvantaged school children may not benefit from such programmes.

We believe that all children have learning potential. But the language, caste, religion, socio-economic diversities do not allow them to pick up age-appropriate ordinary skills in all the domain of development.

Hence, it is essential that the teachers should have a bridge course of child-centred play approach to make disadvantaged children empowered. Just like, a supportive teacher can help them, a software instructor can on occasion make them computer literate and the children can learn to use them effectively. But it needs preparation through child-centred play.

The children need to be empowered to learn. The interactivity depends on the child's ability to interact. The industry believes that all children are capable of it, while this may not be so (Vordener 2001). Human interaction, to which young children naturally respond, is embedded in empathy, compassion and attachment while digital interaction is devoid of it!

Cordes and Muller (2000) insist that computer use is incompatible with young children's normal developmental needs. In fact, as pointed out by Alliance for Childhood, computers could hamper physical, emotional, cognitive development in children. According to this network, one could add social and moral development to the list.

Children learn being fully engaged physically and emotionally in the world around them, and what the computers provide are poor substitutes, it says. Young children's learning is rooted in real experiences whereas computer-based learning is based on information processing or via a mechanist model. It is based on studies conducted on fully-evolved adult brains (Cordes and Muller 2001).

Computer-based learning is said to interfere with self-motivation, imagination and creativity. Computer use is placing the child at risk of rushing through normal development. But there are many who believe that there is no evidence for this. The author of this book, based on her experience of using child-centred play and her clinical experience, believes that computer use in young children compromises normal development in all the domains. The industry, on the other hand, promotes all the new technology despite absence of extensive research on adverse effects on children. After all there was no research to support that in movie theaters, children be kept out depending on the content and films have to be categorised by the certification board as A or U. Can we have such a content-based screening by the tech industry itself?

Social Development

Socialisation by media occurs in the following broad areas.

a. The social context of media use (parental/peer influences).
b. Social relationship and identity development.
c. Effects of violence on social development.

All the above areas need to be evidence-based. Can we please wait for evidence to accumulate?

Collaboration in social context can occur with peers. Friendships can go beyond physical space into very large and accessible possibilities. Scrabble and chess games can be played in the virtual world. Today Zoom conferencing facility makes actual classes possible for the very young as schools are adopting this technology to provide service amidst a global pandemic and lockdown. Yet, this kind of technology is under government cloud as it is open to hacker intrusion.

The effect of TV violence and gaming videos has not been compared. *Actual violence, subtle or otherwise, of Indian language serials have not received any media attention nor have the negative messages of excellently produced TV advertisements.*

Funk et al in 2001 found that 364 fourth and fifth graders showed bad behaviour to measures. Violent videogames are related to low self-esteem (Funk et al 2000) and several other experimental studies have been conducted on gaming content-related violence. For example, Fleming and Rickwood in 2001 found that in 71 children, aged between 8 to 12 years, there was a difference in the level of violent behaviour among children with access to violent videogames and those using more of paper and pencil for games.

To sum up, Anderson and Bushman 2001, analysed 33 studies and indicated significant increase in aggressive behaviour, aggressive cognition, physiological arousal and decrease in pro-social behaviour for children using gadgets excessively. Sherry et al's 2001 meta-analysis of 25 studies of violence against humans and fantasy characters, compared to sports violence found significant increase of aggression in videogames. Increased aggression among children playing videogames with violent context is a significant finding. But short-term long-term impact is yet to be assessed.

Health and Safety

Despite concern over the effect of media and advertising on health, addiction and weight gain, not much research has gone into it. A general suggestion mentioned in the earlier chapter was that online use may be compared to food intake, focusing on healthy food and not over-eating that leads to obesity.

Policy Implications

In 1994, in order to protect children from potential harmful game content, America set up an Entertainment Software

Research Board (ESRB). There are a few age-based ratings. Early Childhood (EC), Everyone (E or KA) Teen (T), Mature (M) and Adults Only (AO) are some. Earlier, only violent contents were included in such scanners. Now ESRB is also an watchdog for sexual themes, inappropriate language, abuse of drug or alcohol are included. These are intended to regulate the industry and promote self-regulation and it is not mandatory to inform the parents of the suitability of the content. However, all gaming and other content has to display ESRB rating.

But most parents do not know or pay heed to the 5 ratings when they buy the games though the industries do display the ratings. Now ESRB has also started to rate the online games and websites. But of the 55 e-rated games, only 64 per cent had mentioned the absence of violence while 44 per cent did not mention violence in their descriptions. When parents rated the same 55 games, 55 per cent of parents rated the content in 3 categories: green light (appropriate for children), yellow light (with caution), red light (inappropriate) for games. May be parent groups can do a better rating exercise than agencies such as the above; parents can perhaps provide better ratings for all the new games as they come up, and share the information among parents and teachers. India urgently needs such ratings.

Online Privacy

External new studies have highlighted use of private data of children for profit by the industry and advertisement. This needs to be put an end to by a policy of monitoring and regulation of the industry and advertising. Overkill, to the detriment of children and putting them at risk of exploitation, by advertisers can be called antisocial behaviour. The industry is indulging in unethical practice and parental consent has not been specifically sought by advertisers. Personal information on children should not be provided at all to advertisers and product makers by any agency collating this.

To summarise, no meta-analysis has been done of successful

interventions. There is a need for individual successful evidence-based interventions with children of different age groups, and survey of organisations offering help across nations. This needs to be promoted.

Guidelines are useful but when you identify a child with a problem related to gadget use, apart from obeying the guidelines how can you help?

Despite mounting evidence of the negative impact of violent games on teenagers, described in all sections of this book so far, Mathew Warren (2019) calls his study, 'Violent delights without violent ends'. It is based on another UK study on a thousand 14 to 15 years old by Andrew Przybylski and Netta Weinstein. Of the 1,150 games participants tested, 2 were rated violent. They measured traits-descriptive behaviour, based on self-report of gamers. The gamers played for two hours a day on average; 49 per cent of the girls and 68 per cent of the boys played violent games.

In India

Let me bring in my experience of aggression in Indian schools, which I conducted with teachers. The WHO had suggested four kinds of aggression in schools, consisting of destruction of school property, aggression against peers, against the teachers and aggression by the teachers.

Most Indian teachers reported sheepishly only the last category was evident in their schools. This has been succinctly summerised by Anagol as, 'The only teaching aid the Indian teacher uses is the stick' (to 'shape' the children).

In my own work in the 1990s, while standardising Achenbach scales to Indian school population, I found that the cut off point for externalising disorders to be used as norms were too high for Indian children. We, therefore, created lower cut off scores based on two standard deviations. Around this time IoT and AI were yet to take off in India.

The reports in general aggression in American schools were greater than in British schools. In India, we had very little aggression among school children two decades ago, before the world of internet dawned and robots existed only in science fiction.

Unlike in the past, at present we see much more of aggression in schools. Aggression in children is multifactorial and cumulative. Exposure to violence in real time and virtual time appear to be similar in impact. This too needs academic attention, after clinical observations. When one finds a ten year old addicted to TV and has oppositional behaviour with parents and aggression with sibling, unplugging the television for a week produces reduction of the aggression; this, to me as clinician, is evidence enough.

New Possible Dangers

Speeding up virtual events, especially in the 5G world:

Can a human brain cope with it?

More importantly, can a child's brain cope with it?

When we view an event in real time, it is slow. It gives us opportunity to evaluate its meaning and impact through secondary reappraisal. The executive functions of the brain do this job. But they need time to evaluate any activity in the broader emotional, social and cultural contexts. Simply by adding EQ (Emotional Quotient) to information processing (computer model of human brain) does not capture the complexity of the brain. By speeding up the outer environment, how does the brain function effectively?

How would a child's brain deal with a sophisticated AI nanny or pet, who can read its mind?

Speed and Slowness

Ultimately, the aim is to speed up all their functions in order to be more efficient at the fastest rate (for example, the present international striving to achieve 5G – fifth generation of wireless communications technologies. It is a measure of speed of data streaming). We **Stop** and **Question**: But **Why**? For whose benefit?

On the other hand, in contrast, over thousands of years, the flora and fauna have evolved at their own pace and as described by Charles Darwin. However, human beings have been exceptional in achieving control over their environment from the human history of tool and fire-making, moving from nomadic to settled life, evolving language along the way, migrating over the entire world. Search for a better life was the ultimate aim. This happened at a very fast pace.

As the humans evolved, their brains and minds evolved at a rapid rate as well. However, in contrast to the present-day requirement, the brains developed slowly and steadily, reappraising every sensory motor input carefully. Speed was not of the essence. *Executive functions located in the prefrontal cortex were the decision-makers.*

In the present century, along with several theories of cognitive development, the *information processing model* emerged. For the first-time, the human brain was seen as a computer, *with capabilities only for simultaneous and parallel processing*. It is now believed even the brains of children can be understood along the same way.

Developmental psychologists adopt information processing perspective account for mental development in terms of maturational processes, in the basic components of the child's mind. This theory holds that humans process the information they receive, rather than merely responding to stimuli. The three stages involved are encoding, storing and retrieving. This, in turn, is linked to sensory memory, short-term memory and long-term memory. This computer stimulated model treats the child as a computer, *overruling the insights of Piagetian Cognitive Theory and the Learning Theories.* While there are multiple theories offered to understand child development, all of them share some insights, useful for understanding the child's mind.

Can the 'scientist in the crib' be compared to a robot?

The reality is that IoT and AI treat young brains as computers and insist on feeding information to manipulate them in the manner they desire. No other theory has deliberately set out to manipulate human mind. Earlier, behaviourists used their theories to modify behaviour to the benefit of the child to some extent. Now we come to the crucial question, what is the likely impact of the speed with which technology is affecting the brain? The answer rests on the theory that the human brain is basically a computer. This theory, in reality, however, offers only a fraction of the possibilities.

Eloise Stark (in *The Psychologist*, 2017) offers an alternate viewpoint that speed is not always associated with good outcomes. She argues that speed is not always beneficial, in fact slowness and deliberateness are equally important. Kahneman (2011) suggested in his book, *Thinking Fast and Slow,* that human mind consists of two competing systems. System 1 is fast, instinctive and emotional. System 2 is slower, effortful, deliberate and conscious and more logical. System 1 is of some survival values, as it is reflexive and fast. One needs slow systems to deal with complex situations. It provides the hallmark of a healthy brain.

Brain and Mind

The examples abound in our daily lives. As against 'fast food', a slow and enjoyable meal is recommended. It leads to greater pleasure and feeling of satiation. Fast eating leads to obesity.

Slow brain process allows cognitive reappraisal. Reappraisal is the regulation of inner states, primarily emotions, through modification of the original emotion. Nietzsche said, 'Those who are slow and know, suppose that slowness is the essence of knowledge'. The common saying 'Slow and steady wins the race' has much meaning embedded in it.

Slowness and human brain neuro-imagining studies by Chang and Gover (2010) have consistently demonstrated that correlations in activity between brain regions evolve over time. Time, therefore, is an important property of the brain dynamics. Spatial patterns are formed, dissolved and formed again over the time. Stork's research into parenting focuses on how slow and fast operate together. While the infants' distressed face may draw immediate attention of the mother, the slow process of long-term attachment occurs. *Parenting is a slow and joyful experience and it should not be surrendered to fast and furious speeding up by IoT and AI.*

Understanding of Science and the Brain

Matt Swayne (2018) brings out the result that overuse of electronic devices is no laughing-out-loud matter. According to researchers, excessive interaction with e-devices may be related to weaker activity in areas of the brain that are key to understanding scientific texts. Overuse of mobiles and smart phones may adversely affect their understanding of scientific information. The neuro-imaging studies at the Penn State Institute of Cyber Science used neuro-imaging to track the excessive use of gadgets, on daily brain activity. In this case, researchers correlated brain activity and the frequent e-device use, such as texting on a smart phone or reading on a tablet. They found that electronic device use negatively correlated with activity in brain areas that are critical for integrating multiple sources of information. Expository texts, such as articles in a science textbook, typically use inter-connected information, which means that material in one part of the text must be linked to information found in another part of the text, especially when reading for the purpose of understanding inter-connected concepts.

In this case, the observation is that if people use electronic devices excessively on a daily basis, that could possibly impair their ability to acquire hierarchical order or structure of scientific concepts, as the readers often must integrate many pieces of information that are arranged in a hierarchy. Just like a person exercises to strengthen certain muscles, the researchers suggest that by using certain areas of the brain and ignoring others, those sections may become stronger or weaker. People who scan or write bits of information too often, may not be building up the brain power to absorb multiple concepts stretched over long, physically written out/printed out articles.

Understanding science is putting the key concepts in different sections of text together. It is not just putting the bits randomly together but to understand hierarchical structure.

The Penn State Institute Cyber Science study group report their findings in a recent issue of Scientific Reports published by *Springer Nature*. The group said, they used FMRI – functional Magnetic Resonance Imaging – technology that monitors brain activity to seek underlying brain patterns that may be associated with integrating information during reading. They simultaneously tracked students' eye-movement patterns to better understand how the readers followed scientific texts.

A total of 51 participants took part in the study. Participants in the study read five scientific articles in the MRI scanner. The articles covered topics in Science, Technology, Engineering and Mathematics, including Global Positioning Systems, electric circuits and the environment.

The researchers found, across all texts, a negative correlation between the self-reported frequency of electronic device usage and activity in brain regions referred to as left insula and the inferior frontal gyrus, or IFG. These brain areas are among the most important parts of the brain for information processing, such as paying attention and understanding language.

The current study builds on previous research. In a 2017 study, the researchers found that people who often used e-devices were less successful on reading comprehension tests after reading scientific texts. The team recruited more than 400 participants from Amazon's mTurk, an online crowd sourcing site, for that study. (Important to note that what is being reported here is not causation but just correlation.)

Middle school children seem to be the best group to start this exploration with, as they enter Piagetian fourth stage of formal operation. Future research may focus on the effect that e-device use has, especially on middle school children, in particular, to understand ramifications of e-devices on learning by comparing tech naïve groups (as our tribal children in my project area) and tech savvy children.

An anecdotal account

Case 12

The Dying Concept of Free Play.

This is a self-report by a former young addict after recovery.

Free play seems to be a thing of the past!

Children in our contemporary times have little or no time for free play, for exploring stuff and just playing what they like!

Their time is mediated and orchestrated by hypercompetitive parents who push them from one activity to the other. My neighbour's child, all of six, is shunted from swimming camps to abacus classes to even a coding for kids camp! Where do children have time to understand and explore their own passions?

Are we so selfish that we want children to just be extension of ourselves and probably fulfil our unfulfilled wishes?

Looking back, mine was a glorious childhood. My family just let me be and do what I liked. I was never forced into any activity. My grandfather surrounded me with story books and comics and I was reading from the age of four. No one told me 'you must read!' I read whatever and whenever I wanted. Sometimes I took up my crayons and coloured or just doodled. I would show these to the family and they would tell me what I could do better. No unnecessary praise, no pushing or goading! I also played around with Lego and built parks and put swings and slides. My grandfather showed me how machines work and I used to be thrilled at the switchboard and lights. Being a chemistry professor, he also showed me how to grow beautiful copper sulphate crystals in test tubes. It was not like formal science, but I really loved it and spent hours tinkering around with his stuff. No one came and told me, 'you are wasting time!'

I was allowed to play outdoors as much as I wanted. There was no curfew on play hours except that I had to come home for milk and a snack and make sure I was not over exhausted. My grandmother had a playschool and so our garden space had a slide, seesaw and a swing. We had a huge *Honge* tree and the swing was like a hammock. My aunt and I spent many afternoons sleeping here or reading Enid Blyton. We often played like Secret Seven or Famous Five and pretended that we were sleuthing for something!

My evenings were spent on the streets with the other kids. We played cricket, catch-catch with a ball, *chor*-police, hide and seek, hopscotch and *lagori*. We always parked our bicycles outside and made sure we cycled in groups every day! Those days the streets had little traffic and it was absolutely safe to cycle. We would cycle from our home. It was exhilarating to cycle downhill with the wind in our hair and clothes!

Some days, the boys in our neighbourhood got out tires and we spent hours chasing them with a stick! My friends would come home to play in our sandpit. We had plastic spades and little buckets. We added water to the sand and pretended to bake cakes. My grandmother would give us Cadbury gems to decorate our mud pies and cakes (which we actually ate). My hair and even my ears would have sand, but it was such fun! My mother never told me not to play in the mud or get my clothes dirty. In fact, I was encouraged to play in the mud, so I would get immunity.

When I look back, I know I learned so much from these games and free play. All of us kids learned cooperation and collaboration through our games. We learned science concepts through our play – like when we would ask my grandfather why we needed so much energy to cycle up hill. None of us were molly coddled or overprotected. If we had a fall and bled, it was ok. We would get cleaned up with Dettol and back again on the streets. If we cycled out too far, it was ok so long as we knew the way to get back home. If we went home with totally muddied clothes, it was ok so long as we showered.

I am sorry for the generations which are glued to their stupid screens (mobile, TV and video games) and missing out on the real fun and learning in free play and games.

Contributed by Namitha Kumar

Indian Scenario

As most of the chapters cover a global phenomenon, I quote extensively this well-known Indian journalist's report, though it covers mostly adults and the youth. After all, these are mostly about Indian parents or youth. Damayanthi Datta's cover page article in the *Outlook* magazine in September 2019 is aptly titled 'The devil on your palm'. She says that as India enters the digital era, a mysterious relationship between technology and human behaviour grips the nation, creating strange disabilities and often leading to horrific deaths. She lists out the following disorders linked to technology.

She has interviewed several experts. Neurobiologist

Dictionary of Malaise

FoMo or Fear of Missing Out	Online Gaming Addiction
Phantom Ringing Syndrome	Cyberchondria
NOMO Phobia OR No-Mobile Phobia	The Google Effect
Cybersickness	Technoference
Facebook Depression	Truman Show Delusion
Internet Addiction Disorder	

Sumantra Chatterji explains the neuroplasticity of the brain which enables it to recognise and re-engineer itself. This happens in response to the environment, behaviour, thinking and emotions. Advances in the brain scan technologies reveal internet addictions and gambling has remarkably similar effect on brain. Both trigger one of the reward chemicals, namely dopamine and hijack the brain influencing motivation and judgment. Mobile phones and social networking sites place people in stressful situations. The stress comes from the unprecedented volume of personal information. This leads to unfavourable comparison leading to negativity.

According to the World Health Oraganisation (WHO) *'Digital disorders are hugely under-recognised in India'*. According to Rajesh Sagar of AIIMS Delhi, 'It is fast emerging as India's newest lifestyle disease'.

The advice is that you can re-wire your brain by being aware of your dependence.

- Spending time in healthier activities
- Meditation
- Face to face socialisation
- Meaningful relationships
- Physical exercise
- Learning new things
- Sleeping adequately

All the above will make you a better spouse, companion, employee and most importantly good parents.

My Reflections

1. I, as a clinician, believe that parents should form self-help groups for their children and not seek online solutions.

   Entry into real world starts with real encounters among people of a supportive group. This could be done along the lines of AA. In my experience, parents' group meetings on the mental health problems of their children have been very enlightening. I have found that parents themselves offer solutions to difficult behaviours of their children. Some parents feel relieved that their own child is not as difficult to manage as that of other parents.

   We also concurrently run a 'Philosophy for Children' programme. We propose to use this forum to discuss screen addiction and real play.

2. Establishing centers to help internet addiction. *In Bangalore, the National Institute of Mental Health and Neurosciences offers a SHUT (Services for Healthy Use of Technology) clinic for internet addiction. This could be created across the nation.*
3. Legal ways to restrain unlimited online access by tech industry and advertisers, who steal and use private data. If they do not self-regulate, there is a need to take legal recourse. After all, the powers of the tobacco lobby has been clipped and they have been made to pay for the damages to health caused by them, as a result of lawsuits against them, claiming huge compensations. If we have the proof, we can win the legal battles. But it has to be done at the government level.

Following is the description of sessions with parents conducted at our Child Guidance Centre (CGC) on the first Saturdays of every month:

Parents' session on the first Saturday of every month was started on the 7th July 2018 and continued for a year. Ten sessions were conducted till July 2019. Initially, these sessions on first Saturdays were planned for the parents of children with hyperactivity and learning difficulties, educating them about the problems and their management. Later it was decided to include all parents who come to seek counselling at CGC, as a self-help group.

Structure of Parents Sessions Stepwise

i. Self-introduction of parents and sharing their challenges as parents.
ii. Introducing the working pattern of CGC
iii. Deciding about the topics of discussion according to the challenges put forth by parents.
iv. Psycho education about the topics (expert opinion) by the facilitator of the session.

v. Interactive discussion
vi. Learning/feed-back by parents

Objectives

1. Creating awareness in parents about the problems faced by children.
2. How problems are different from child to child and how dealing with them too is different.
3. Knowing the challenges faced by other parents often help in reducing anxiety in most of the parents.
4. One thinks that only their problem is big, but when they see others' challenges, they feel relaxed and try to cope up with their problems smoothly.
5. The approach to parenting is holistic as children may have multiple problems (disorders) and these often overlap.

Thus, parents get an opportunity to share their challenges in a group, a Self-Help Group. However, it is a self-contained one session self-group, as often new group members form 2/3 of the group. The rest may have participated two times or three times. In India, group participation on an outpatient for the same group over stipulated number of sessions is almost impossible. Each time the group has some new members and some old members.

Through the sessions, so far, a diverse range of challenges have been encountered. Some of them are:

1. Difficulty in reading, writing and maths
2. Poor academic performance
3. Hyperactivity
4. Lack of concentration
5. Emotional issues
6. Poor socialisation
7. Addicted to screen – TV, Mobiles, computers etc
8. Irregular Food and feeding habits

9. Disturbed sleep pattern
10. Punishing the child
11. How to make reading and writing enjoyable
12. Attention difficulty
13. Importance of family time
14. Lack of confidence
15. Sibling rivalry
16. Stubbornness
17. Shyness
18. Social withdrawal
19. Behavioural issues
20. Peer pressure
21. Difficulty in caring because of nuclear family setup or in a joint family set up

There was even a case where the parents complained that the 'child always plays' and that was the main issue that the parents perceived as a problem.

Each and every challenge above mentioned were addressed by the facilitator as to what may be the cause? What may be the reason for continuation of the issue? And how it can be resolved?

As the sessions were interactive in nature, the parents talked of a number of causes, reasons for continuation of the problems and also came up with solutions in dealing with the issues. Examples were:

1. Issues with the parents
2. No friends to interact and play in neighbourhood
3. Screen addiction
4. Pampering and over-indulgence from parents or otherwise
5. Parents too busy in their career
6. No time for children to play as there is too much pressure from academics
7. Comparison at various levels, at play, at school, at

family gatherings, etc

8. Pressure from school
9. Temptation from colourful foods outside
10. Inconsistent disciplining
11. Parents themselves becoming the rule-makers and rule-breakers
12. Parents who can afford give anything to their children
13. Maximum one child or two children in the family, and families mostly becoming nuclear
14. Lack of play area
15. Parenting is not easy as the children are exposed to too many things in the real as well as virtual world
16. Dilemma to decide between what is normal and abnormal
17. Strict parenting
18. Placing parents' burdens upon children
19. High expectations from the child
20. Problems in education system
21. Punishment, most parents consider it essential
22. They believed that the children are lazy and hence not performing up to their potential

One important question which emerged from the facilitator that made all the parents speechless was, 'You all say that you are facing problems due to your child, what problems are your children facing from you?'

All the parents present in that session thought deeply about this and it was an eye-opener for parents, that they were the role models for their children and what they sow – they shall reap.

Facilitator/s added few more points about causes for the problems, such as

- Mental state of the mother during pregnancy.
- Characteristic is passed through genes/hereditary.
- Variations in the mental and physical development.
- Consumption of junk food.

- Inability of children to process multiple stimuli.
- Gross and fine motor development varies from child to child.
- Imagined good parenting.
- Giving more importance to academics rather than the overall development of the child.
- Criticising children which leads to anxiety, memory problems, fear, low academic performance, emotional issues and also sometimes school refusal.
- Difficulty in studies is commonly shown by behavioural issues.
- Emotional stability.
- Punishing – both verbal and physical.
- Lack of self-care by parents.
- Too much dependence on technology.

It is not that one size fits all. It is according to the varying requirements that a tailor makes dresses to fit each person. The strategy adopted for each child vary according to the age of the child, disorders, temperament in the context of family, neighbourhood and the school.

So, each and every child is unique by himself. Good observation and support from the parents, accordingly, help to make a child bloom in the perfect manner. Understanding, accepting and acknowledging the child's problem will make the life of both parents and child, easier.

Dealing with the problem is as important as the problem itself. Some of the major solutions which came out through the sessions for the above-mentioned issues were:

1. Children learn well through play.
2. Unconditional love towards children will have positive impact in the behaviour of a child.
3. Making reading more enjoyable through stories and introduce academics gradually.
4. Making writing enjoyable, first by developing fine

motor skills through activities such as drawing, colouring and tracing. The only rule to be followed is to appreciate and not to criticise the child at any point.

5. Play the age-old traditional games.
6. No comparison of one child to another.
7. Let the child learn to feed by himself by letting him enjoy his food.
8. Avoid screen time by involving child in more play activities.
9. Being calm and consistent with child.
10. Practice yoga and pranayama (breathing exercises).
11. Let the child to be independent. Most Indian parents of middle class do not like it.
12. Encouraging the positive aspects/behaviours of the child and ignoring some of the negative ones and addressing some of the negatives in a positive manner by talking it over with the child.
13. Good anger management by parents will have positive effects on children
14. Children have more energy and it has to be channelised in a right direction.
15. Assure that child is supported, but do not yield to whatever the child unreasonably asks for something.
16. Consistent disciplining is needed.
17. Cutting down dependence on technology.
18. Cutting down media/screen time.
19. Make a timetable and follow it.
20. Negotiating effectively and following it consistently.
21. Planning sufficient movement and physical activities.
22. Parents also have to work on their screen time and self-discipline.

Play is the best solution to most of the issues faced by children which is lacking in the present day, due to various reasons such as the present education system, lack of play

area and time, parents being busy in their own work, absence of siblings at home and now, a pandemic.

Thus, through various sessions, awareness was created in parents that the major problems in the children were due to *inconsistent parenting*. Small changes from parents' side make a major change in the child's behaviour. Parents often are astonished by their small behavioural changes resulting in dramatic improvement and even full recovery on many occasions.

Parents Feedback

Parents understood the importance of observing the following behaviour protocols:

- No comparison to other children.
- Understand the child.
- Not to force the child, it will be better if the child does anything with interest.
- More importance to be given to activities and not academics.
- Give quality family time to child.
- Free play and other activities help the child to perform well in academics also.
- The problems faced are looking smaller now and can be resolved by themselves.
- Communicate well with the child.
- Be a good role model to the child.
- Be with children, connect and bond with them.
- Look at things from child's point of view also.

Over the ten sessions, there were some common impressions, positive feelings among the participants, they felt more relaxed and happy to get solutions from within the group.

All the ten sessions had the following common components:

- Inculcating good feeding habits.
- Sleep patterns need to be negotiated, shifting to earlier hours.

- Screen time and its management.
- Importance of play.
- Arts and crafts as mean of self-expression.
- Storytelling and reading and their importance.

Apart from guiding in the existing problems, basics of conduct and emotion disorders, ADHD, SLD and its effects and management were also covered in some of the sessions. Importance of diagnosis of the problems was also emphasised. Information about various facilities available for remediation, treatment, referral, suitable school placement, exemptions given by government for children with problems such as SLD programmes was also given.

Many of the Parents guided through these sessions have even mentioned that they have changed their family dynamics which is working out well and are very much satisfied. Hence, they have discontinued from the regular counselling sessions also.

One session stands out among the ten and directly concerns the theme of this book. Hence, a detailed account is given.

Screen Addiction

As screen or gadget addiction came through in almost all the sessions, and also posed as a major problem, facilitators made it a point to address these concerns. Counsellors spoke at length on the causes, effects and how to resolve the problem of screen addiction.

Few important points communicated were:

- The brain development is rapid in the early developmental stages. During this time, all the five sensory modalities of the child has to be activated. This is achieved by our physical presence and interaction and not by gadgets like phones, tablets, etc.
- Harlow's experiment – explains that the baby monkey needs mother, not just for feeding but for the warmth and comforting touch. This gives the child, a feeling

of security. When we interact with our children by talking, singing, playing, telling stories, etc, all the sensory modalities are activated, which is not possible with a gadget.

- The child gets attached to that person who is physically and emotionally close to him/her the most often. Usually, it is the mother or any other care giver. If the gadget is replacing that human figure (singing lullabies and telling stories) then the child gets attached to that gadget and not to human beings.
- People who create these gadgets are known to keep their own children away from technology and gadgets. So, we have to think why we are giving it to our own children?
- Feeding with gadgets: *One of the worst habits observed in India these days is feeding the children while they are with the gadgets. By doing this, we are giving a message to the child that eating is something not enjoyable. In addition, for some strange reason, mother feels guilty if the child does not eat well. When the child senses the mother's anxiety, he starts to make more fuss to gain her attention.* So, we are pairing it with gadget, which appears interesting. Instead of this, allowing a toddler to play with food and eat on his/her own, share a family meal etc. will make the child love food. Also, eating together with family will promote pro-social behaviour. The fuss Indian mothers make feeding the kids need to be seen to be believed. Even a fussy ten-year-old gets fed by the mother!
- Screen time and its impact on behaviour – It is another important factor to be understood. Studies show that increased screen time results in more aggression. Most of the contents on media are inappropriate for children. And the children repeat words, actions and behaviours that they are exposed to without actually understanding them.

- The games they play on phones and internet expects them to be fast, furious and very aggressive. Such games make children less empathetic. These children will not be able to feel for others and find it difficult to have attachment with others. All these will make them feel that they should be the winner in whatever they do and cannot take defeat and failures in life.
- It is understood that spending more time with screen will cause anti-social behaviour in children. Whereas, more time in activities with peers and family members promotes pro-social behaviour.

Some of the outcomes from the parents were:

- As parents, we need to spend more time with children.
- Encourage them to participate in real activities that promote their all-round development and well-being.
- We need to show them affection, compassion and empathy.
- We too need to manage our addiction to screen and encourage children also to do so.

(Team: Drs Geetha and Malavika Kapur and compiled by Sindhu HR and Arathi Rao)

Psychosocial interventions are essential for all developmental mental health and educational difficulties. Paying attention to only the complaints which bother the child, parents or teacher is not enough. The child should be viewed and understood from a holistic perspective. The approach should be child-centred. A single disorder or multiple disorders need detailed history taking; building of strategies vary depending upon each child's needs, parenting and school issues. Symptom removal alone is not enough. Overall development needs to be promoted and the child and the family should be happy with attachment, bonding and effective communication and quality time together. Let us go back to the basics of childcare.

Protect your child and it is your duty. Set limits and introduce happy real time activities. Have regulators to restrain unethical practices of IoT and AI.

REPLACE VIRTUAL REALITY WITH REALITY IN THESE DIFFICULT TIMES

We have a double jeopardy on hand. At the time of writing, there is exponential growth of Covid 19 as well burgeoning of online platforms. Increased viewing of child pornography and domestic violence are proofs to the negative effects of viewing violent content in the pervasive nature of what is sent online, often free. The negative fallouts related to internet invasion is completely ignored and has been heralded as a great boon in this difficult time. It has actually been declared 'the shining future way of communication' among the entire humanity. It is important that research is conducted in an unbiased way into the good and the bad of taking over of the education system by online platforms.

The obvious fallout is the exploitation or neglect of the weak and vulnerable because of age, gender, race, social class, minority status and of course, the disability.

While the elderly are at risk of Covid 19, the young are vulnerable as there are predators ready to pounce on them with violent games and other violent and addictive content.

There is also an insidious effort to promote online teaching not as a temporary solution but as a permanent one. This is the most serious crisis that faces education unless sanity prevails. This is just like making all the daily basic needs eventually available on line. Who benefits from them? Encouraging digital India is to gain control over the people. Who benefits from them economically? Socially? Politically? We need the answers for these questions. The IOT and AI behemoths, marketing executives, the Credit Payment mode operators, and of course the pharmaceutical companies. Everyone would be offering every thing free of cost initially as bribes but these will eventually cost a bomb.

I believe all children are born creative but teachers or gadgets with one way communication destroy their creativity. A child does not need a YouTube to teach him/her how to live with nature in harmony and learn from it.

IT TAKES A VILLAGE TO RAISE A CHILD

NOW THE VIRTUAL WORLD RAISES THE CHILD

LET US LEARN FROM CHILDREN HOW TO RAISE THEM
AND RECLAIM THEIR CHILDHOOD

References and Resources

Adair Catharine Steiner. *The Big Disconnect Protecting Childhood and Family Relationships in the Digital Age*. amazon.com.

Anagol J (2003) Compulsary Primary Education Opportunities and Challenges, Booklet 2. Pune, Indian School of Economy.

ASER (Annual Status Of Education Report, 2008-2016.

American Academy of Paediatrics (2011). Policy Statement. Media Use by Children Younger than Two Years. *Paediatrics*, 128 (5), 1-6.

American Academy of Paediatrics (2013). Children, Adolescence and the Media. *Paediatrics* 132(5), 958-961.

Ban of Corporal Punishment in Schools (2010). Ministry of Women and Child Development. India.

Bowlby John (1969). *Attachment and Loss*, Vol 1, Attachment, New York, Basic Books.

Brooks Kim (2018). *Small Animals in the Age of Fear*, Fat Iron, Macmillan Publishers.

Centerwall BS (1994). Television and the Development of the Superego: Pathways to Violence. In *Children and Violence* (Eds). C Chiland and Young GT, Vol.2, The Child in the Family: NJ Jason Aronson Inc.

Chomsky Noam (1965). *Aspects of the Theory of Syntax.* MIT Press.

Chomsky Noam (1968). *Language and Mind.* Harcourt Brace and World.

Conradie DP, Heineken M and Botha MP (1987). The Effects of Television Violence on Television Naïve Pupils, a follow up study of 5 years, Prelora, Human Sciences.

Datta Damayanthi. Demon on your palm, cover story in *Outlook* magazine,16 September 2019.

Doan P, Andrew and Strickland, Brooke (2012). Hooked on games: The lure and the cost of video games and Internet addiction. *FEP International.*

Donnely Laura. Children who spend more than two hours a day on Smart phones seven times more likely to develop ADHD. News, *Telegraph* 2018.

Donnely Laura (2018). Duty of Care. https: www/telegraphco.uk News 2018,10,31, Britain. medicalising children rather than bring them up properly.

Dunkley Victoria, Electronic Screen Syndrome. An Unrecognized Disease? *Psychology Today*, July 23, 2012.

Eron LD and Huesmann LR (1984). The Control of Aggressive Behaviour by Changes in Attitudes, Values and Conditions of Learnings. In *Advances in Studies of Aggression.* (Eds.) RJ Blanplank and DC Blanch and Orlando Fla, Academic Press. pp 139-171.

Eubanks. Virginia (2018). Automating Inequality. *How High-tech Tools, Profile, Police and Punish the Poor.* amazon.in.

Fleming. MI and Richwood, DJ (2001). Effects of violent and nonviolent video games on children's arousal, aggressive mood, and positive mood. Journal of *Applied Social Psychology Psychology*, 31,2047-2071.

Funk JB, and Buchman. JN (2000). Preference for violent

electronic games, self-concept and gender differences in young children. *American Journal of Ortho Psychiatry*, 70,233-241.

Freed Richard (2015). *Wired Child*, South Carolina, Creative Space, Independent Publishing Platform.

Goleman Daniel (1995). *Emotional Intelligence*, New York Bantam Books.

Gopnik Alison, Meltzoff Andrew N and Kuhl Patricia K (1999). *How Babies Think.* The Science of Childhood, London: Weidenfeld and Nicolson. (The American edition has the title; *Scientist in the Crib.*)

Harlow Harry. Nature of Love. American Psychologist, 1958, 13, 673-85.

Hart Betty and Risley Todd. (1995): Early Catastrophe: The 30-million gap by Age 3, Americal Educator, Spring: 4-9.

Jing Shia, Renwicka Rebecca, Turnerb Nigel E, Kirsha Bonnie. Understanding the lives of problem gamers: The meaning, purpose, and influences of video gaming. University of Toronto, 160-500 University Ave, Toronto, ON, M5G 1V7, Canada Centre of Addiction and Mental Health, 33 Russell Street, Toronto, ON, M5S 2S1, Canada. *Computers in Human Behavior*, 97 (2019) 291-303.

Joy LA, Kimball MM and Zabrack ML (1986). Television and Children's Aggressive Behaviour. An Impact of Television: A National Experiment in Three Communities (Ed.) TM Williams, Orlando Fla, Academic Press. pp.303-360.

Kapur Malavika (1997). *Mental Health in Indian Schools.* New Delhi, Sage Publications Private Limited.

Kapur Malavika (2006). *Learning from Children What to Teach Them*, Sage Publications Private Limited.

Kapur Malavika (2011).*Counselling Children with Psychological Problems*, New Delhi, Pearson Ed.

Kapur Malavika (2016). Psychological Perspective on childcare in the Indian indigenous health systems. Springer India Pvt Ltd.

Karadaras Nicholas (2016). *Glow Kids*, New York, St Martins Griffin.

KentaroToyoma (2015). *Geek Heresy*, Rescuing Social Change from the Cult of Technology. http//www.amazon.in. Geek-Heresy-Kentaro-Toyoma/dp/161039528x

King Daniel L, Delfabbro Paul H, Gainsbury Sally M, Dreier Michael, Greer Nancy, Billieux Joel. Unfair play? Video games as exploitative monetized services: An examination of game patents from a consumer protection. Perspective *Computers in Human Behavior*. 2019, accepted July 2019.

Kohlberg L (1984). The Psychology of Moral Development: The Nature and Validity of Moral Development. An Essay on Moral Development (Vol. 2), New York, Harper and Row.

Menschand Gustavo and Talamud Illan (2013). Wired Youth: Social World of Adolescents in the Information Age. New York, NY. amazon.com.

http/Annenberg.usc.edu/mews/annanberg-agenda screen time

Mohitt TE, Arseneault, Besky D, Dickson N, Hancos RJ, Harrington et al (2011). A Gradient of Childhood Self Control Predicts Health, Wealth and Public Safety. Proceedings of the National Academy of Science of the United States of America, 108(7) 2693-2698.

Newson E (1994). Video Violence and Protection of Children. *The Psychologist* 7:6, 272-274.

Piaget Jean (1929). *The Child's Concept of World*, New York, Harcourt, Brace and World.

Piaget Jean (1970). *Science of Education and Psychology of the Child.* New York, Orion Press.

Robinson, TN, Wilde, ML, Navracruz, LC, Farish, Hyde lK and Varady, A (2001). Effects of reducing children's television and video game use on aggressive behavior: A randomized controlled trial. Archives of Pediatrics and Adolescent Medicine, 155, 17-23.

Rideout J Victoria, Vande Water, Elizabeth A and Wartella A Ellen (2003). Zero to Six: Electronic Media in the Lives of Infants, Toddlers and Preschoolers. (PDF) from Ed govt.

Rorschach H (1927). Rorschach Test-Psycho-diagnostics, based on perception (10th Edn) Cambridge MAA, Hogrefe Publishing House.

Sharma Yash Pal Learning from children what to teach them. In Education Dialogue (2005),2,(2)273-275.

Skinner BF (1953). Science and Human Behaviour. New York, MacMillan.

Stark Eloise. Is Slowness the Essence of Knowledge? The Psychologists, July 2017, 38-39.

Stavropoulosa Vasileios, Anderson Emma Ela, Beard Charlotte, Qasim Latifi Mohammed, Kuss Daria, Griffiths Mark. Addictive Behaviors Reports; A preliminary cross-cultural study of Hikikomori and Internet Gaming Disorder: The moderating effects of game-playing time and living with parents. (2019) 100137.

Thomas A and Chess S (1977). Temperament and Development, New York, Bruner, Mazel.

Uhis Yalda T, Machkiyan Minas, Morris Jordan, Garcia Debra, Small Gary W, Zgourou Elini – *Computers in Human Behaviour*, Vol.39, October 2014.

US Commission on Causes and Prevention of Violence.

Vygotsky LS (1984). *Thought and Language* (A Kozulin Trans). Cambridge, MIT.

Wang Y, Hummere T, Konenberger W, America, Scientific

Assembly Meeting, Chicago Illinois, November-December 2011.

http://archiv.rsna.org/2011/11004116 html

Moiser K, Mathews V. One Week of Violent Video Game Alters Prefrontal Activity. Radiological Society of North America.

Watson JB (1930). *Behaviourism* (Revised Edition). New York, Norton.

Wood Charles T, Skinner Ashcley Cockrell, Brown Jane D, Brown Callie L.

Janna B Howard, Michael J. Steiner, Andrew J Perrin, Cary Levine, Sophie N Ravanbakht, Eliana M Perrin. Concordance of Child and Parent Reports of Children's Screen Media Use. Academic Pediatric Association.19, No.5, 2019.

Cordies C and Millar E (2000). Fool's gold: a critical look at computers in childhood. College Park MD: Alliance for childhood. Retrieved April 25, 2002 from http:/www.Allianceforchildhood.net/projects/computers/computers_report_fools_old_contents.html

Ramirez Lisa. Dignity for all students Act (DAS) http;/www/ liberty uk12>org department and services>Student services.

Scigel Daniel and Harzell Mary www.danseigel.com/uploads human% attachment (pdf) Centre for Culture Brain and Development.Copyright 2011.

Wartella E, O'Keefe, B and Scantlin, R (2000). Children and interactive media: A compendium of current research and directions for the future. Menlo Park, CA: Markle Foundation. Available at http://www.markle.org/news/digital_kids.pdf.

https://news.psu.edu/story/583253/2019/08/12/research/brains-trained-e-devices-may-struggle-understand-scientific-info.

http://www.netlingo.com/emailsh.cfm

https://www.huffpost.com/entry/is-screentime-bad-for-my-child-5-myths-about-kids_b_58e54e83e4b0ee31ab953446

Erika R Cheng and Tracey A Wilkinson, Agonizing over screen time?

https://www.nytimes.com/2020/04/13/parenting/manage-screen-time-coronavirus.html

Anderson CA et al, Screen time and physical violence and youth behaviour, *Pediatrics*. Aa publications.org: contentSupplement-2, Nov1, 2017.

Jenson I, Boyce BF and Picket W, Screen time and physical violence in 10 to 16 year old Canadian youth. Int J Public Health 2012:57(2) 325-31.

https://www.theguardian.com/technology/2018/may/31/how-much-screen-time-is-too-much-for-kids-parents-advice-children-digital-media.

https://theswaddle.com/effects-of-screen-time-on-children/

https://www.nytimes.com/2018/12/10/health/screen-time-kids-psychology.html

https://www.forbes.com/sites/jamiemadigan/2019/08/05/new-research-how-much-screen-time-is-bad-for-kids/#7726498d4d30

https://www.vox.com/2015/3/31/8320233/time-spent-with-kids